THE MOTIVATION STATION

An Essential Guide to Becoming Your Greatest Version

By Pita Taufatofua

The Motivation Station

COPYRIGHT

The Motivation Station

An Essential Guide to Becoming your Greatest Version

Copyright © 2018 Pita Taufatofua

First Edition

ISBN: 978-0-6485516-0-7

All rights reserved. No portion of this book may be reproduced or transmitted in any form or by any means without permission from the author or publisher, except as permitted by copyright law.

For permissions contact: TeamPita@outlook.com

www.Teampita.com

Disclaimer

The purpose of this book is to provide information for its readers and is strictly for educational purposes. Should you wish to use some or all of the ideas contained within this book, you are taking full responsibility for your choices, actions, and outcomes. You understand that the Author and or Publisher is not engaged to render any psychological or any kind of professional advice. The reader should consult with trained professionals in any matters relating to his/her physical and mental health, and well-being. The Author and the publisher do not assume and hereby disclaim any liability for psychological, physical, emotional, financial or other damages or loss resulting from use of the information within this book.

Pita Taufatofua

To My Mother

Who taught me that we can achieve anything
we put our hearts and minds to.

To My Father

Who taught me that helping others is the true
meaning of life.

The Motivation Station

TABLE OF CONTENTS

Introduction 6
Motivation 11
The Mechanics of Motivation 16
My Life Purpose 24
Laziness 41
Procrastination 48
The Comfort Zone 57
Remove Negative People 63
Negative Thoughts and Depression 77
The Mind vs. The Body 103
Alcohol, Drugs, and Porn 126
Lust, Sex, and Love 147
Nutrition 153
Exercise 168
8-Step Motivation Guide 178
Fear and Nerves 227
When Everything is Going Wrong 239
Fail Happy and Forgive Yourself Quickly 251
Always Finish — Always Finish Strong 257
Gratitude 262
About the Author 266

Introduction

*"Within each of us is a great treasure — its value priceless, and its potential limitless.
My name is Pita Taufatofua, and I will be your guide..."*

Within the pages of this book, you will find information that will change your life. If motivation and self-growth are what you seek, you will turn the last page a new person. This book will not be a source of your motivation. Instead, it will light the fire within you; one we all have, the fire of accomplishment and purpose. Rather than seeking external things to inspire you, you will find that the inspiration you desire will come from within.

With your newfound knowledge, you will unlock the motivation you need to become your greatest version. But first, a little about me.

Like many of you, I come from humble beginnings. From this average start in life, I have accomplished many things in what seems a short amount of time. I wasn't born with much sporting talent. In fact, I was one of the underdeveloped, awkward kids at school who couldn't make a sports team.

Despite this, I am now one of a handful who has qualified and competed in two Olympic Games, Summer, and Winter, in two unrelated sports. My first was Taekwondo. My second Olympic games, I learned a new sport, cross country skiing, and reached an Olympic level within one year.

I have spoken publicly on motivation and self-development for people from all walks of life. I have worked in shelters for over fifteen years and helped create one of the most successful self-development programs for homeless youth in Australia. This program has taught thousands of disadvantaged youth to break the cycle of homelessness, giving them practical skills to live fully and independently. This work along with my Olympic achievements led me to become the first UNICEF Goodwill Ambassador for the Pacific.

Some would say I am motivated. But despite my accomplishments, I wasn't born that way. In fact, most of my adult life was a less-than-perfect picture of motivation. I lived in my mother's basement through a lot of my twenties while I worked to become an Olympian. It was my dream, and I had no idea how to achieve it.

For the twenty years it took to become an Olympian, I had no sponsors and no financial help. I worked full time, trained full-time, and also studied for an engineering degree, again, full-time. I didn't do it this way because I was necessarily motivated, but because I had no choice and needed to survive. Working gave me an income to get through university and to help fund my sports training.

I come from a family of seven children but lost my sister, Wendy, to leukemia when we were young. My father was a farmer, and my mother was a nurse. We were poor financially with eight of us living in a one-bedroom house on a little farm on the tiny Pacific island of Tonga. What we lacked in money, we made up for in love; I was blessed with a supportive family. And from the support and lessons from my parents and role models, I was able to navigate my way to success and my Olympic Dream.

Eight of us lived in this little house before a cyclone took it.

Through years of struggle, frustration, injury, and pain, I learned everything I now know about living a motivated life. Working in homeless shelters with countless clients over many years, I saw just how powerful the human spirit can be. That despite the most challenging circumstances, a person can achieve great things and overcome the toughest of life's challenges. Studying why humans choose one behavior over another was my drug.

I wasn't satisfied going through life guessing, I had to know what drives us to do the things that we do. During the many months I was stuck in bed due to Taekwondo injuries, I read and studied everything I could about motivation and human development. At that time, I could barely walk due to my injuries, but my mind could still learn. I then took everything I learned and started applying it in the homeless shelters where I worked. I was refining my knowledge. To my surprise, there were certain things that not only worked well but were reproducible, client after client. I started to apply what I understood from my parents and my interactions in the homeless shelters, along with my struggles, to become an Olympian, to create a comprehensive plan on how to live a motivated and happy life. After all, what is motivation without happiness? I went through the pain and absorbed the lessons over years of trial and error.

From those years, I have condensed everything I learned around the topic of motivation into this book. It has been over twenty years in the making. Behind the words are many tears, much labor, and many great memories. With these lessons learned, you will be able to fast track your progress by understanding my mistakes and successes. As the words leave these pages and absorb into your mind, know that I am here sharing this motivation journey together with you.

How is it that I get motivated, and how is it that I always seem to stay both motivated and happy?

In the pages to follow, I will teach you exactly how I apply motivation to my own life. From it, you will get a strong understanding of how motivation works, and you will see exactly how you can apply it into your own life quickly and effectively. I will use many examples from my work with homelessness, my childhood growing up on a farm in Tonga, and from my sporting quest to become an Olympian. The lessons in these examples are applicable to any area you seek to improve, whether that is finances, relationships, and/or self-belief, etc. My examples may be based largely around sports, but the spirit of each story is universal and applicable to whatever your pursuit is. Read with an open spirit, and you will absorb so much more. Allow yourself to feel the stories, and the right lessons will find you.

There will be many times where I repeat key points in the text over and over. I do this purposefully the same way I would teach a Taekwondo kick, through repetition. This repetition will jump-start new and positive mental habits, as you read.

Each of you will get different lessons from these pages. If you take just one thing from this book that changes your life, or that you apply every day, then my goal will be accomplished. Years of dedication to human development will have all been worth it. If you are excited to become someone who is both happy and motivated, then read on. I am excited, so let us begin.

Pita Taufatofua

Motivation

"Living a motivated life will bring you growth, with that growth will come happiness."

Let's not waste time. You are here because you need more motivation and you need it now. But do you even know what motivation is?

As a young adult bumbling my way through life, I didn't understand what motivation was. I had many positive habits that naturally helped me achieve goals, but I also did a lot of negative things that did nothing but sabotage my efforts with finances, relationships and time management and delayed my success. I was still running a lot of the negative programming that had inadvertently entered my life. I was careless with money because I never had any, and therefore didn't understand how to use, invest, and save it. I had never learned about time management and was whimsical with time, always arriving late. On a positive note, I was persistent at everything. I never gave up. But persistence alone wasn't always enough. It was like trying to cut down a tree with a hammer. Persistence meant I would eventually succeed. But it would take more time than it should. That hammer needed to become an axe. I am thankful for it all, the negative and the positive habits.

It would have been great to be a young kid growing up pursuing my dreams and knowing exactly how to do it, but I had no clue. In fact, I didn't even realize what motivation meant until my mid-twenties. More importantly, I had no idea how to harness its power to help me achieve things that I wanted to achieve. As a young Pacific Islander, some days I would run away from school and go fishing with my friends. I didn't know what drove me to prioritize fishing over education, and I didn't care. All I knew was that fishing was more fun than school, and that it made me feel good. As I grew wiser, I learned that I could not just do the fun activities that gave instant gratification without also finding a way of doing the activities that would benefit me in the long run. My fishing days soon became balanced with education, after my grades had dropped. I got my first taste of what motivation, or being determined, meant. It wasn't just about doing what we wanted to do, but also what we needed to do in order to benefit us in the short and long term.

Let's start with what motivation does.

Motivation affects every aspect of your life. Every action you take — whether you think about it, conscious, or don't, subconscious — has an element of motivation in it. If we think of every part of our body as being a living, connected entity with its own reasons for existence, then we can even break down body actions into motivation. Our heart beats because it must transport blood throughout the body. It is *motivated* by our survival. Our lungs expand and contract our whole life; they too are *motivated* by our survival. When we raise our arm to shake a stranger's hand, it is a gesture of friendship or peace. We are "motivated" to raise our arm and expend energy to maintain peace and safety.

If motivation serves a survival/beneficial purpose, then it would be fair to say that a lot of the decisions we make should also serve as survival and beneficial purposes. Yet this isn't always the case. Sometimes we do things that are bad for us. We eat the wrong food, spend money we don't have, and consume excessive amounts of television or social media per day. Whereas, what we should be doing are things that improve our lives and the lives of others.

So why is it that different people have different levels of motivation? Why is it that given very similar circumstances, one person can excel at a task, whilst another will crumble or not even attempt a task that can benefit them? The answer, as you will see, comes down to our habits, fear, priorities, history, and a lack of understanding about how we, as individual human beings, work.

If every action we take is dictated by motivation, then it makes complete sense that being motivated will have a profound, positive effect on the quality of our life. If we are able to treat what we do consciously, the same way that our body treats breathing on a subconscious level, then our life will dramatically change for the better.

Imagine if exercise, eating healthy, saving money, or spending more time on things that enrich our existence, was no longer a conscious decision fraught with excuses but a sub-conscious daily action. Imagine the impact that would have on your body and mental health. How would you feel if you didn't have to think about doing something positive, you just did it? Are there areas of your life that this would benefit?

This book is a seed. It isn't the fruit. The fruit will come from how you implement the information I have written for you. The world is full of information that isn't implemented. Someone who struggles with weight may have the knowledge that certain foods are bad for them. They may even hate the health implications of being overweight. But they eat these foods anyway. Knowing something is not enough; acting on it is what will make the difference. Action beats knowledge. The key to unlocking a motivated life will be how you decide to use this and any information you learn. If you put in the work daily, the seed of knowledge from this book will become the fruit of *being motivated*, and your life will improve dramatically.

The following chapters are laid out like a ramp. They start slowly to ease you into an understanding and progressively speed up in content and intensity. This is done very deliberately. If I were just to give you some steps to employ in your life, there is no guarantee that they will stay. If, on the other hand, you start building the context and foundation that is required for a motivated life as you read, then the information will be retained. This is because you will have created the blueprint needed through your own understanding and individual circumstances. My stories and examples are exactly that, mine. You cannot copy my struggles, but you can see where they align with yours and use the lesson. This is about you creating your own story and understanding of life.

Some chapters will overlap. Different people may find the key they've been searching for in a different section of this book. Your aha moment may come at any time or in any of the chapters. If this is the case, then apply that lesson immediately into your life. Don't wait. With that said, I encourage you to read through all sections. What I have found in life is that sometimes we find answers where we least expect them.

With my understanding of motivation, I now know exactly why that young kid ran away from school to go fishing. I know that the instant joys of only doing what I wanted to do would not serve my bigger dreams. It's extremely liberating knowing exactly why you do everything that you do. It takes away a lot of the anxiety and guesswork out of life.

If you thought motivation was just about learning a few new tricks, then you would be mistaken. The majority of your motivation will come, not just from you learning new things, but also from you unlearning old habits and releasing past trauma. Being motivated is about understanding yourself.

The Mechanics of Motivation

"We can create habits by repeating a task. The more we do them, the less we need to think about doing them"

I want to start by congratulating you for making it to the next chapter. Many people purchase a book and either don't open it or never make it past the first chapter. Your inspired life has taken a strong start!

Let's talk about how motivation works. People have it all wrong. They assume that it is something that enters their life and stays. I wish that were the case, but it isn't. They think that people are either motivated or lazy by nature. The truth is that motivation is impulsive, kind of like a cat. It comes when it decides and leaves when it decides. And if we try to force it to stay, it claws at us and escapes. We can't use force, but we can train it to want to stay. By changing our way of thinking, we are better able to train our motivation cat to come into our lives more often and to stay longer. Once we can do this, we find that long term motivation isn't in fact motivation but purpose and positive habits. It is this purpose and these habits that will carry you through the winters of life.

Have you ever had a New Year's resolution? Or did you see something online or on social media that inspired you? Why is it that within a few weeks of starting your New Year's resolution you are back to old habits after failing miserably? Why couldn't you stick with that diet or finance plan? That motivation you had at the beginning of the year was like our hungry motivation cat coming for its New Year's meal and then leaving after it was done. In order for it to stay, we must train it to rely upon us for a meal every day, not just every so often. We do this by creating a comfortable and safe environment for the motivation cat to enter and leave at will. We make the path for it to be so easy that it has no choice but to come into our lives. This is also known as creating a habit. By feeding our motivation daily, it stays with us. But we must feed it daily.

How do we foster an environment for motivation to stay? In the following chapters, you will find a wealth of knowledge plus eight key steps for creating a motivated mind. One of these steps is creating a living environment based around what it is that you want to achieve out of life. If you have health and fitness goals, then having a kitchen full of unhealthy food won't nurture your motivation. Temptation without a disciplined mind is a sure way to fail. We need to train our mind first before we test it with temptation. If you want your motivation cat to stay, you won't fill the room with an angry dog. And so, if you want a motivated mind, you won't allow it to be filled with negative or tempting thoughts.

A lifetime of Taekwondo and martial arts training has taught me the self-discipline needed to create a motivated mind. That said, that experience has also taught me that life isn't always fair nor is it meant to be. But through its ups and downs, the disciplined mind always triumphs. I've seen this in practice in the shelter work and in training for the Olympics. Discipline allows a single set of principles and values that you decided upon to control your life. When this happens there is no inner conflict, you are running one clear program that doesn't compete with another. Motivation comes when we apply self-discipline to create positive habits that replace our negative habits. If you want to become more motivated, you will need to train your self-discipline. You don't need to do years of martial arts training to do this. Instead, you will do it step by step, little by little.

I learned a form of martial arts called Hapkido. It is a deadly art used by the Korean Special Forces. When I started, I was in my first year of university in Australia after spending two years in a boarding school far away from my home in Tonga. I had nowhere to stay, and so my father asked an old friend of his if I could sleep in his garage while I attended university. Each day, I would walk a few kilometers to my Hapkido class located in the neighboring area. I didn't have any money, so buying a bicycle was out of the question for that first year. One thing Hapkido teaches you is self-discipline. Our club was run by my very tough Korean master also known as Sabumnim. He was very kind, yet at the same time, extremely disciplined. A tough breed of Korean warrior well trained in the deadly art of Hapkido. One day I arrived late for class after a delay in finishing at my university. Not coming to class would have been better for me than arriving late. Being someone who always shows up, I wasn't about to miss class.

My punishment for arriving late was simple. I would stand with my two feet up against the wall, my hands behind my back and my head on the ground forming a tripod. I had to stand this way for the whole two-hour class while the other students did their training. After ten minutes, the blood would rush to my head, and I would pass out. Once I remembered where I was and could see again, I would have to resume the position. This happened for the whole class. At any time, I could have stopped, grabbed my bag, and just left. But I was stubborn and giving up wasn't in my vocabulary. By the end of the class, I had a terrible headache, but my self-discipline muscle had been strengthened. Although to this day, I occasionally arrive late to events, I never once arrived late to my Hapkido training after that. I learned that motivation required an element of stubbornness and tenacity. You couldn't just give up on the motivation cat because training it was hard. You had to keep going.

The easiest way for us to do something consistently is to create pathways in our mind which make completing the task easier. A mind pathway is a simple way of doing something that doesn't require much motivation. An example of a mind pathway would be anything you do with minimal thought, such as opening a door. You have done it so many times that you don't need to be motivated or think about doing it. It just happens. Have you ever driven a car and completely zoned out, not remembering all of your driving actions for the last twenty minutes? That's an example of a more complex mind pathway. Through years of driving, you were able to take a once complex task and put it into your subconscious mind, making the task effortless. Your mind pathway for driving was well laid out. Now, this isn't to say that's the safest way to drive, but it works. It also highlights the point that quite complex tasks can be completed relatively easily with enough training, once they become habit.

In Taekwondo, we would train the same kick over and over, year after year. As an instructor, I would often see students roll their eyes when we would make them lean up against a wall and throw the same roundhouse kick for a full two-hour session. This, to the untrained eye, was a boring and tedious use of time. After all, most of the students already knew how to throw a roundhouse kick, or at least that's what they thought. There is only one sure way to test if the skill you have learned is part of your subconscious, and that is to test it under pressure. When competition time came around was when the countless hours of repetitive training would really shine. Whilst other competitors would stand there planning their next move, my students and I were always ready. We would throw roundhouse kicks with perfect timing, technique, and speed in a way that the opponent never knew what was coming. Truth is, half the time neither did we. The kicks were so ingrained in our subconscious mind that we rarely had to think about them; they became a reaction. And in the heat of battle, we could rely on that training to get us through, even when nerves and fatigue would try to hold us back.

In February 2016, when I first qualified for the Olympics, I won the final match of the qualification tournament by a golden point. This is when the first person to score a kick wins the match. In my case, this was the deciding point that allowed me to become an Olympian. The person who loses that point goes home and has to wait another four years to try again. Because the scores were tied in my final match, we went to a golden point round. It was Tonga vs. New Zealand. In the opening seconds of the round, I threw a kick that scored and cemented my place as Tonga's first ever Taekwondo Olympian. What was interesting is that I walked out of the ring and told my coach that I didn't even remember throwing a kick. I had no idea what had happened. My mind pathway was so well trained that in the most nerve-wracking of situations under extreme pressure, I was able to perform. Had I left it down to thought and thinking about when to kick, then I would possibly have lost the match. The habit of kicking without thinking, created from repetitively training that roundhouse kick, is the reason I qualified and became an Olympian.

So how do you create pathways in your mind? Like anything, through repetition, practice, and work. The more you do it, the easier it becomes. What are the first things you do every morning after you wake up? Chances are you have done these things for so long that the pathway to taking these actions is clear, at least in your head. Now imagine if these actions aren't beneficial for you, such as eating a large sugar-filled breakfast. Every morning, you would have created a mental pathway making it easy for you to do a task that leads to a negative outcome. Eating a sugar-filled breakfast for years cannot possibly be good for your long-term health, but you've done it anyway, and so you continue to do it with little resistance. You aren't consciously thinking about that breakfast, as you've probably eaten the same foods for so long. Any task that has a clear mental pathway will be easy to do, regardless of whether that task provides good or bad results. You can see how it is essential to be aware of our mental pathways and our everyday tasks resulting from them. You can also see how motivation to achieve great things comes from having clear mental pathways aligned with your goals.

So long as you are relatively safe from harm, the reptilian, or survival, part of our brain doesn't care what you do. It's up to you to make a conscious effort to train the brain in what it should be doing. Remember, the mind that we are born with is programmed in what it thinks its task is. This brain wiring is only partially specific to each individual. It wants you to survive, consume food, and procreate or make babies. Procreation allows our genes to be passed on. It is an evolutionary hack that allows us to, in a way, live forever. We need to tailor how our mind does things to what we actually want out of life. Rather than having life or our random upbringing train our brain, it is time for us to make conscious training decisions to teach our mind how to function in a way that's more beneficial for us. We need to become the master of our subconscious mind.

We train motivation, first and foremost, by understanding its benefits to us. Just like the motivation cat, we nurture the environment for it to stay, and we welcome it back every time it makes an appearance. Our habits that we created whilst we were motivated drive us forward towards our goals. Like the cat, if our motivation feels comfortable enough to stay, then we will live a motivated life, where completing tasks is second nature. But if motivation decides to leave for any period of time, then we will still have the habits and mind-pathways that keep us moving forward until it returns.

For anything, including motivation, to be second nature, we must train it. Not eating that bowl of ice cream, consistently putting away money — however small, waking up early, and walking for five minutes a day; all of this is training self-discipline and our habits. While each task may seem small or trivial, it isn't necessarily the task itself that brings the benefit but training yourself to do the task consistently. You are training your motivation muscle, and thus your mind-pathways, just by doing that small task. When the heat of battle comes, and temptation and laziness are knocking at your door, you will be well equipped to throw that golden-point kick that gets you the life that you deserve.

The key points are that we must turn motivation into a habit by repeating the tasks that we need to accomplish, however small. This creates a mind pathway much like driving without thinking that will make any task simple. Our goal is to make it so easy for the motivation cat to be a part of our life that it visits us often, and when it leaves, our habits keep us moving forward.

My Life Purpose

"The tallest towers have the deepest foundations."

Goal — The goal of this chapter is to help you zoom out and view your life in the context of a bigger picture. It will help you understand the importance of having a world view and developing deep, strong foundations from which to base your motivation and goal accomplishment journey.

When I was twelve years old, I stood along the road with thousands of other kids in Nuku'alofa, the capital of Tonga. The first Tongan Olympian to get an Olympic medal ever, Paea Wolfgramm had just arrived in the country, and we were excited! Kids lined the streets for twenty kilometers to wave and cheer for him as he was driven on his float. As he passed by, I remember him waving at me while I held a big P sign for his name Paea while three other students held the other letters. In that moment I told myself I would become Tonga's first Olympian in Taekwondo. The question is, had that moment never happened, would I have become an Olympian? Was it part of my life's purpose as created by God or the Universe or was it a random set of events that had me create my own life purpose? Would I still have become an Olympian if I was sick at home that day? I like to think it was my destiny, but the truth is I don't know. Life doesn't come with a manual. Whether destiny or self-created purpose, it really doesn't matter. It was aligned with who I was becoming, and nothing was going to stop me from making it happen. Becoming an Olympian took twenty years, and what a ride it was.

It would be easy for me to tell you what you need to do to get off that couch and *be motivated*, but it won't last or be fulfilling without the information in this chapter. If you want a lifetime of motivation, then you must do the groundwork first. The groundwork is the hardest part but the most rewarding and long-lasting. If done right, motivation will be easy. Welcome to the chapter on life purpose.

A search for a greater understanding of the meaning of your life will be the single greatest gift I can give you from this book. If you read this chapter and then go on a personal quest of self and Universal discovery I can but guarantee you a motivated life. The reason I have achieved much and am consistently happy isn't because I was born lucky, it is because I put in the work to figure out or create my life purpose and my understanding of the universe. I am at peace with my understanding of how the world and universe works, and by embarking on this quest, soon you will be as well. This for some may be the hardest part of the book but also the most necessary. Once you complete this chapter, the sailing gets easier. It may be confronting, but don't be afraid. Tackle it like you should any challenge, head on.

Have you ever seen the tallest, grandest buildings ever made? They don't start with the builders laying bricks on soil but with the builders digging deep into the earth. The higher the building will be the deeper they will have to dig to lay the right foundation. The problem with digging is that no one wants to do it. It requires removing a lot of dirt and travelling in the opposite direction from the building. To build a foundation, you go down but to build a building you go up. No good building was ever built without first digging down. It is the most necessary step. The deeper the root goes, the stronger the tree grows.

But we are not here to build buildings or plant trees, we are here to get inspired. How does it relate? The strength of your motivation is proportional to the depth of your foundations. It isn't by chance that the most successful/happy/motivated people in life also give deep philosophical advice about life. Their questioning, and understanding, of their place in the Universe stays strong. They are always seeking answers. They are content in seeking answers, whether they find them or not. If you want to be motivated to do great things, you need first to build your foundation. Your foundation is your safe place or your series of beliefs and values about life, it becomes your unwavering core. Now there are people who are highly philosophical but not action-oriented, and there are those who can take action but lack philosophy. What I am referencing are that the greatest most motivated people have both, action and their form of universal understanding. They think about the big picture. This is the kind of motivation you should strive for. These are the kinds of results that will keep your life inspired and fuel your passion for more.

Your foundations should be strong and unwavering in times of crisis. And they should be built long before crisis hits. This will give you peace of mind that you can do anything and that you can take the risks required to achieve great things because you will always have a safe place to fall back on and recover from if things don't go to plan. If you haven't built your foundations and are currently in crisis then fear not, they can also be made during turbulent times. Just know that the tree will never be strong if its roots don't run deep, so your motivated life will be as strong as your foundations.

Sometimes we find that there are people who have seemingly lucked their way into success or fortune.

Certain families have been born into money. Or certain sports stars were born genetically gifted. Some people were born with slightly better hormone regulation and thus are generally happier, and some were born into good loving families. And then there were those of us who were born with next to no perceived head-starts in life. Everyone was given a different and random set of circumstances from which to start life. None of this was within your control. And then throughout life, they were given a different set of challenges that they would need to overcome in order to grow. Some people would spend their whole life complaining about their circumstances whilst others would find ways to celebrate both their circumstances and their challenges. When we accept the reality about the circumstances we were given, whether fair or unfair, we free ourselves to find the best way to make our life better. We understand that we are only partially in control of what happens to us externally, but we are in full control over how we react when these things happen. That is to say, we should strive to be in control of ourselves internally.

My head-start in life was a loving family. My challenges included growing up very financially poor and isolated in the middle of the Pacific Ocean. I had severe health issues as a child which I overcame as an adult. Being part of a large Polynesian family meant seeing many loved ones pass away. My sister, Wendy, died when I was only five. I remember the adults wailing and sobbing uncontrollably at her funeral. Later that week, I woke my mother up one night, because I too was wailing and sobbing, "Oiaue Wendy," in my sleep. Oiaue in Tongan is an expression of shock or grief. I really wish I had gotten to spend more time with her, but this wasn't to be. None of these things, good or bad, were within my control.

Polynesians interweave humor into painful situations as seamlessly as they weave their mats made from the bark of pandanus trees. This is done to lessen the pain of what may be happening. One summer's day we were out at sea on a tiny boat travelling to the small island of Kotu in the middle of the Pacific Ocean. Suddenly, the boat died. A crankshaft bearing had failed meaning the engine couldn't be fixed until we got to dry land. Hours went by as the captain tried fixing it. He was whistling away as though he knew something I didn't. I was starting to get worried. We could barely make out land on the horizon and there was nothing we could do. No safety equipment, no cell phones. As a child we often look to the adults for signs of danger or panic. None came.

As nightfall arrived, I asked the captain if we were going to be ok as we were broken down in the middle of the ocean. He looked at me and laughed. I could see he was missing his four front teeth. I asked him why he was laughing at me, and he said everything will be ok. "We have six-weeks' worth of water." I didn't know what was so joyous about six-weeks' worth of water, so I asked my father who looked at me and smiled. He said, "That's how long it should take us to drift to Fiji (a neighboring country) where they can rescue us." This was Polynesian mentality — humor in times of stress. Luckily for us, a boat eventually came by and offered to drag us to the island. We were spared six weeks of being out at sea.

I learned very early on from my culture and parents not to take life too seriously. This was great advice as it meant I was mostly at peace with whatever was happening as it happened. I wasn't depressed about my past or anxious over my future. This gave me freedom.

Your set of challenges and your circumstances were largely out of your control as well. Whether random or from a master creator it's the hand that you were dealt. Accept it, and you will be at peace with it.

Laugh and joke about everything, and your life will change for the better. This is one of my greatest lessons from our Polynesian way, and one I would love for you to embrace. Tongans are notorious for laughing about everything. We have a habit of remaining upbeat in times of struggle. This is one of my foundational cores and one which gives me strength. We allow ourselves to mourn the sad times, but we don't stay there for long, and neither should you.

Stuck at sea with Captain Manase.

So back to our foundation. Before we address the steps like writing goals and *why statements*, we need to lay our foundation. Simply put, our foundation asks the important questions about life.

These questions can differ slightly for different people, but they create your world view, how you see the World. They include my three big life questions.

-Where did we come from?

-Where are we going?

-What is the meaning of life?

People are scared to ask these questions because they require a deeper level of thought. Thinking deeply also means possibly opening parts of our brain that some would rather keep shut. A question as big as, 'What is the meaning of life?' is a terrifying and overwhelming prospect for many of us. For others, it is a question that we have never even thought of. The answer to this question will be as unique as the individual asking it. There may be common themes, but the answer will be painted by a person's current knowledge and life experiences. If a certain person has the answer that life has no meaning, then that could be very confronting for them, especially if they don't re-frame their understanding into something positive.

For someone who says life has an abundance of meaning then this question could give them joy. Whatever your answer is, it should be liberating knowing you are creating a strong deep foundation just by asking questions.

By asking questions that are bigger than us, we allow ourselves to see a bigger picture. We can zoom right out of our life, and when we look back in at our little selves sitting on this little but beautiful planet, something amazing happens. Our problems which consume us and steal our motivation become small and yet our greatest Dreams become attainable. The bigger picture allows this to happen.

Sometimes in life, we get caught up in our own problems and challenges. If you're like me, you might have found that your motivation needed a boost, but you weren't quite sure where to find one. What has happened is you have zoomed so far into these problems and challenges that you've gotten tangled in the details. This chapter is about zooming out. Releasing yourself of all the details that consume you about your life and zooming so far out that you see yourself as a little spec. All of a sudden, the details that consume you lose their significance and all that matters are your overall place and purpose in this grand Universe. It should feel extremely liberating zooming out from your problems. Take some moments and just enjoy the view and while you're there, enjoy the feeling.

* * *

So where did we come from?

Were we created or did we evolve from something? Or we can look at it from a more recent perspective. Where did my parents come from? Why are they the way they are? How has this influenced me in becoming who I am? Am I repeating cycles of incorrect thought passed down from my grandparents to my parents? I love the *where did we come from* question because it allows us to step right back and out of our own problems. We can become so caught up in the detail of our lives that we forget to see the bigger picture. From the zoomed out view we see that our problems are only really small. Everything was here before us, and everything will be here after us. We only have control over what we do while we are here. We are a part of a master tapestry that is nothing short of grand.

Where are we going?

This can be our spiritual or religious beliefs around what comes after we pass on. Or it could be what is the direction of us as a species or a planet? What we are doing is trying to draw a bigger picture about our future direction. By having a belief system, we ground our self. We don't have to have an exact answer and in fact, most of us won't. What we do want to do is ask the big question and start thinking about the answer. We don't want to think about the answer in a doom and gloom manner, but, in a similar way, a child looks at a butterfly and wonders where it is going. It is more a curious, questioning way of thinking. Your motivated life requires you to think far bigger than yourself, which allows you to become un-phased by day to day problems.

The *where are we going* question removes a lot of anxiety as you address it initially and then become okay with your answer. If you are constantly unsure about the future, you will live in anxiety. If you are okay with whatever the future brings, then you are free to live in the present moment.

The final and most important foundation question is:

What is the meaning of life?

This looks at why we as people are here. Is there a greater purpose for us and what could it be? Or on the other hand, does life have no meaning other than to exist and do the best in the time that we are given? The meaning of life question is one of the biggest philosophical questions you will face. It also overlaps with the *where do we come from* and *where are we going* questions. You don't have to have the answer but think about the question. Let it sit in your subconscious mind as you go about your day, and the answer will reveal itself when it is ready.

We have asked the big questions about life, and you are powering through, well done! But we're not out of the woods just yet; we still have some foundation building to get through. We still have some digging to do.

Unlike physical building foundations, we can slowly add to our life's foundations as we learn more about ourselves and our universe. Be brave and ask yourself these questions and do it in a light-hearted way. The answer may not be apparent straight away and may take years or a lifetime but open your mind up to seeking that knowledge. The goal isn't necessarily to find an exact answer but make it one of your quests to seek an answer. I have been asking myself these questions since I was a child. I am motivated not just for a better life for myself but for a better life for everyone on this planet. Step back and see the big picture.

Once we have answered the three life questions, we can now ask the big ambition question from which our goals and a lot of our happiness is derived:

What is the meaning and purpose of my life?

Some people may know the immediate answer to this while others will slowly discover it. It is our overarching life purpose that will dictate our motivation and success. When everything is going wrong, and motivation and results start to drop, then it is this question and our answer to this question that we can come back to, to reground us. This is our fallback position, our safe place.

When I polled my social media followers, I had over ten thousand people respond. I asked them to choose answers to the *what is the meaning of my life* question. Of those, the majority (60%) fell into the first group which was, "I don't know my life purpose, but I am searching for it." The second largest group (30%) was, "I know my life purpose," and the smallest group was, "Life has no purpose," (10%).

Which of these three groups do you fall into?

I don't know my life purpose, but I am searching for it.

I know my life purpose.

Life has no purpose.

You may be in the 10% that fall into the third group of *life has no purpose*. This can be a scary place. After all, if there is no purpose to our life, then what chance do we have of doing things that motivate us to improve a purposeless life? The great thing about people in this category is that they can do one of two things. They have a blank slate from which to find or create life's meaning, or they can find freedom in their belief that with no meaning comes no pressure or expectations; this could be liberating for some. Now, this isn't to say they can do what they want, as society still requires laws and rules. But they can be content in knowing that they at least have a foundation.

That said, I would always challenge them to reframe their understanding so as to move into the first group of not-yet-knowing their purpose. It's very easy to assume life has no purpose when everything is going wrong, and internal conflict constantly batters you. I believe that all life has purpose, energy and life force. We are here for a grand reason whether we know what that reason is or not.

For those who haven't yet found their purpose in life, the best thing to do is to take your best guess. Your best guess may seem vague for creating a life purpose or foundation, but it is, after all, you building the absolute best foundation with the knowledge that you have at that time. If you don't know the purpose of your life, create a positive life purpose with what you do know, and you can adjust as you go. Our best guess is us saying there are certain things I am more drawn towards and certain things that really don't sit well with me. My best guess is an acknowledgement that I don't have all the information yet, but I can still create a foundation with the information I do have. What you will find is that the deeper meaning of life and your life purpose more often than not is about other people and your contribution to them.

Some life purpose examples may be:

- My purpose is to change the world
- My purpose is to be a great parent for my kids
- My purpose is to become the best football player ever
- My purpose is to have a farm that provides vegetables for the people of my village
- My purpose is to paint beautiful paintings that touch people's hearts
- My purpose is to help the sick
- My purpose is to create beautiful music

It doesn't matter what this purpose is so long as it creates positive outcomes for you and those around you and is something that you feel naturally drawn towards. If you are of that group who feel that *life has no purpose*, then you can still create "your purpose." I knew since I was twelve years old that I wanted to become an Olympian, and despite life's challenges, that feeling never left me. I guessed at the time that my purpose was to become an Olympian. Throughout my years, I have expanded that purpose to be bigger than myself. Now my purpose is to use my story of how I became a dual Olympian to help others achieve their dreams. I also want to find ways of looking after and bettering our planet for future generations. While knowing your purpose early on is rare, there are many who do. Others will find or add to it along the way. For you, this may be music or finances or, for some people, painting.

Pita Taufatofua

What has always drawn you towards it? What is your best guess for your purpose in life? Write that down and read it every morning for a week. At the end of the week see how it feels. Do you still feel drawn towards that purpose, or do you need more time to help it grow?

When I was twelve years old, I wanted to become an Olympian.

Imagine your life purpose is a plant; nurture and feed it. Once it blooms, it may become like a beautiful mango tree. If you want more flavor in your garden, then plant and nurture another great purpose, and now you will also have a banana tree. There is no rule saying that you may only have one purpose. So long as your foundations are strong, and you nurture your aspirations, then you will go through life creating a beautiful, garden-of-life purpose from which to nourish your soul and for others to enjoy.

Sometimes our purpose will grow and change as we change. If for example, you feel your purpose was to become the world's greatest football player, and you reached an age where you felt that was no longer possible, that may confuse you. I mean, you felt so drawn towards it. This is where a lot of people get stuck or have a mid-life crisis. How they thought their life would be, and what it has become may be completely different. This can feel very discouraging and even heartbreaking. They question everything they have ever known about themselves and their purpose. They say things like, "Was that really my purpose? Why didn't I achieve it? Were all those years wasted?" And they may even fall into depression and self-sabotage as they feel unworthy of even themselves. The truth is that no time was ever wasted, so long as you did what you loved, or it moved you closer to what you wanted. Even the things that didn't work out gave you lessons that will continue to help you throughout life.

You may not have become that famous singer or football player, but if that had been your passion and purpose at the time, then that journey would have been filled with amazing moments and people. This in itself is a win. Maybe the pursuit of that dream was your purpose for that time. When you start to view things from a perspective of everything that happens to you is positive, then your life changes. This isn't to gloss over the harsh realities of challenging experiences but to accept that they happened and actively seek out both the lessons and the good things from them. Life is harsh enough without you adding to it with negative thinking.

Life moves in seasons and the transition between seasons can be scary, or they can be exciting depending on your view. You may not have become the world's greatest football player, but now you have the opportunity to become the world's greatest coach, father or writer etc. Remember the ones who did become that famous musician or football player also go through the exact same process of change as all of us. In fact, for them, the seasonal change can be even more heartbreaking as they transition. You only have to look at tragic Hollywood tales of drugs and depression to see this. Imagine being the world's greatest football player for many years, and then suddenly, no team wants you. That is a bigger fall than the rest of us will have to take.

With great purpose also comes great challenge. This should not discourage you but prepare you. But with a positive mindset, even that football athlete who fell from greatness can smile their way into their exciting new season of life. Our purpose can change and grow with us.

To tie it all together, you must first build your foundation before you build your goals and motivated life. Your foundation asks crucial questions about the meaning of your life and your life purpose. Once you have this foundation, it will be your fallback option when everything in life is going wrong. Rather than hitting rock bottom, you will bounce off your foundation. It is your safe place and will dictate your direction in your day to day tasks. Spend some time to read and find a purpose that is true to you. It is okay not to know exactly what your purpose is just yet but make it a part of your life to continue searching.

Well done, I am proud of you, you made it through the heavy stuff. It's time to clear that soil out of your fingernails now that your foundation is well underway.

Laziness

"No one is born lazy; children read and run and play. We accumulate and learn unproductive habits, but like all habits, we can also unlearn them and relearn productive ones."

Goal – The goal of this chapter is to learn about laziness and to highlight ways that we can change our way of thinking about it.

There is a big difference between someone who appears lazy and someone who procrastinates. Notice how I said *appears lazy* as opposed to *is lazy*. We will get back to this. But for now, let's focus on general definitions. Laziness implies that someone doesn't really want to do something, whereas procrastination says that someone doesn't really want to do something now. Laziness means they would rather do nothing or remain idle than expend energy to do a task. On an arbitrary motivation scale, procrastinators sit slightly higher than people who appear lazy; make no mistake, they both sit in a place we don't want to be.

So let's talk about laziness. As a youth counsellor of fifteen years, I worked with thousands of challenging young people from all walks of life. One thing that really stuck out to me was an incident I witnessed one evening that most people would simply overlook. I was observing another youth worker interact with a teenager, asking that teenager if they could change the channel on the television. The teenager slumped on the couch, defiantly refusing many times, and coming up with every excuse possible. As a keen observer, I noticed that the teen had no interest in watching what was on TV but also didn't want to expend the energy in that moment to get up and take two steps to change the channel. Now some may say that the teen was just being a typical defiant teen resistant to authority and direction, but the truth was, was that that young person had a strong respect and rapport with that specific worker. He, at that moment, just genuinely didn't have the drive to change the channel.

Now the worker, assuming the young person was being defiant, proceeded to call him lazy and predicted that he would struggle through life if he continued his unmotivated ways. The worker thought the kid was lazy because he applied his own definition of laziness to the teen. Right then, he had forgotten that there was a whole myriad of reasons that the teen was in a homeless shelter. Changing a channel was the least of this young person's problems or priorities.

Later that evening, and in the middle of winter, the young person who had no money, no phone or access to transport, disappeared from the house not to be seen until three days later. He had hitch-hiked, jumped a train, and then hitch-hiked some more for half the night to get to his drug supplier to get his drug fix. He then slept in a park for two nights, so that he didn't come home under the influence of drugs. Despite his drugged state he didn't want to jeopardize his accommodation with our shelter. Returning under the influence would result in him being expelled from the program as it put other young people at risk. Putting the drug element aside, would you call this young person lazy or resourceful and motivated? From a getting-something-done perspective, he exhibited signs of extreme motivation.

The problem wasn't that he was lazy, but that he was motivated in the wrong direction. He was motivated to do something that would harm him in the long term in exchange for immediate, short-term gratification. I, being the observant worker that I was, waited until he had come down off his binge a few days later and proceeded to give him positive reinforcement. I let him know that he was actually a very motivated young person, who had the respect not to jeopardize his accommodation, and then proceeded to ask him how I could help him find better channels for that motivation. The young person acknowledged his drug addiction and asked if there were steps we could take to help him.

What I found through many years with many clients was that people only changed when they wanted to change. We could never change someone who didn't first bring an element of wanting a better life. I linked this young person up with a drug rehabilitation program. I then spent every shift I had exercising with him to show him the benefits of training. It took months of hard work and some relapses, but eventually, the young so-called *lazy* teen was able to kick his drug habit and focus on becoming a personal trainer. He found that the benefits of training helped him swap out drug addiction with a new healthy addiction, exercise.

We have to be very careful not only about how we label others but also ourselves. People will live up or down to the expectations we put upon them, including laziness. If we keep saying that we don't do something because we are lazy, even if in the context of a joke, then soon we will believe it and subconsciously act to fulfil it. The language we use with ourselves and others is extremely important and helps to determine our outcomes; guard it carefully.

The above example shows us that with laziness, more often than not, someone just doesn't prioritize a certain task high enough on their action list. The immediate short-term discomfort of doing work outweighs the delayed long-term rewards of that work. There is no immediate gratification, and so the so-called *lazy* person chooses not to do a task. In order for this instant gratification mentality to be changed, we first must acknowledge its existence. Expose it for what it is, and then get to work on making long term happiness a higher priority than short-term instant gratification. Moving towards our life purpose must be more important than a quick fix that moves us away from our life purpose.

Ultimately, each person is the captain of their own ship. If they perceive their life as being happy and fulfilled, then who are we to impose our pressures and lack of contentment upon them. Yes, they may not be achieving their absolute potential, but they are happy, and if being *lazy* brings them happiness, then so be it. You will waste precious energy trying to convince someone who is adamant about not changing to change. Focus on growing yourself, and others will see the benefits and hopefully start their own journey to lead a more motivated life.

From an evolutionary standpoint, laziness could be seen as a form of energy conservation. Back when we were hunter-gatherers, we had much less access to food than we do now, and so conservation of energy was vital to survival. The only time we needed to work was to hunt or gather food, improve our social standing, procreate or to adventure. Now whilst some of these things may still be the case, the mechanisms have definitely changed in modern times. We can hunt and gather from the comfort of our home with internet-based food and product delivery. We can engage in adventures through online gaming whilst also improving social status through social media, again from the comfort of our home. We don't need to expend nearly as much energy as our evolutionary ancestors in order to survive. Hence the rise of increased couch laziness.

But there is a flip side to modern laziness. When someone feels lazy, they will spend a large amount of that couch time thinking about what they could or should be doing. That feeling won't go away. They say, "The devil makes work for idle hands." If we aren't actively doing something that progresses us, then we open ourselves up to elements of depression and also negative habits. Humans must move, we need to be progressing at something to really feel fulfilled.

Movement and completing tasks releases brain chemicals that increase happiness. Dopamine, serotonin, and endorphins are some of these happy chemicals and are released in much higher amounts through activity and real accomplishment. This isn't to say that sitting down in front of a computer all day won't achieve your goals, as for many professions, it will. What it does say is that we will need to balance inactivity with activity to optimize life's positive outcomes. In eastern culture, there is the concept of Yin and Yang which states that everything must be in balance. If your work involves periods in front of a computer, then you should balance this with activity.

This doesn't mean that eight hours of computer work requires eight of movement, it's not a time-balance problem. The physical activity could be completing a house chore or a ten-minute walk. It could be a training session at the gym or a yoga class. It is very hard for us to see the importance of doing a physical activity when we are wrapped up in our work. It can feel like a waste of time, especially if you have a deadline for that work. The problem isn't that we prioritize work; it's that we neglect the activities that balance the work. The deadline that we target often is just followed by another deadline and another deadline and so on, and so forth. And before we know it, we've gone days or weeks or months without exercise. The irony is that exercise will not only reduce your stress levels but also improve the quality and enjoyment of your work. As your blood moves through your body from exercise, you'll notice your mood improves and your creative thoughts become freer to express themselves.

If you find that you are spending too much of your time stuck on a couch or in bed wasting the day, then it is time to move. Literally, time to move. That is all it takes, movement. Get up and do something physical. It could be a five-minute walk or a simple task that you enjoy. Your goal is movement because with movement comes momentum. And with momentum comes results. You don't need to complete the big task that is weighing you down, you just need to move. And you do it as many times as you need to create the new habit. Whether it takes days, weeks, or months.

You may intuitively know that you can't stay on the couch all day, but you feel stuck. Understand that even though you may be feeling lazy, you aren't a lazy person, few people are. They are just lacking purpose, direction, and progression habits. The fact that you are reading this already tells me that you aren't in the group who doesn't want to change but in the group who does want to change.

Monitor your lazy times. Do you feel lazier in the morning and find it hard to get out of bed or is it a mid-afternoon thing? If you find most of your lazy time is after lunch for example, then after lunch is when you need to have pre-arranged things happen. This could be a yoga class or a business meeting, or maybe even, that is when you go shopping for groceries. Remember there is a big difference between lazy time and you physically just needing a rest. If you're getting a good amount of sleep a night, then chances are the only midday rest you need would be meditation or a power nap — not hours on the couch staring at a wall.

In summarizing, and putting aside dietary challenges, no one is really lazy they are just lacking the right purpose and direction to their life. If you find you are spending too much wasted time stuck on a couch or in bed, then it's time to move. Laziness is self-perpetuating. The more time you spend doing nothing, the more you ingrain in those habits of doing nothing. Make small movement-based tasks to get you out of those lazy times. Your goal for laziness really is nothing more than small movement. If you have written out your goals for the day, then that small movement will lead towards them. Once you start moving, then bigger tasks will flow from there as momentum is built.

Procrastination

"Procrastination is a thief of time and thus life. Remove it, and you will increase the quality and effective length of your life."

Goal — The goal of this section is to help you understand some of the reasons why you procrastinate. We then look at what you can do to help stay focused on a specific task.

Procrastination differs from laziness in that there is a desire to complete a task but at a later time. Procrastinators use excuses such as "I will start tomorrow," or, "there's still plenty of time," or "I have other things to do," etc. They fill the time needed to complete the task with other less important tasks. They run through a justification process within their mind that allows them to do this with minimal guilt. Have you ever gone to write an assignment or do exercise and ended up cleaning the car or playing video games instead? You just may be a recovering procrastinator.

The procrastinator believes that they will complete this task within an allocated time frame. It's seen that, more often than not, they do in fact complete the task within the said time frame. The issue isn't that they didn't complete the task, but that they did so at a much lower quality than they could have achieved had they planned better.

I spent a lot of my adult life as a procrastinator. That is until I recognized that it was stealing time from my life and preventing me from achieving great things. In my early twenties, I would sit down to a university assignment, and four hours later, would find myself watching baboons fighting on internet video sites. Why is it that I was so easily distracted? Why couldn't I focus on the important task that needed doing? Well for one, baboons fighting was more interesting, and on top of that, I also much preferred doing what I wanted to do over doing what I needed to do. The weeks-away assignment deadline gave me no immediate work pressure. This certainly wasn't healthy and led to many low-quality assignments being submitted at the last minute. As I write this, I laugh. Being an expert in motivation, I should be telling you how I never wasted a moment of my life. That isn't true. Part of real growth is accepting our shortcomings and being able to find ways to change them. We only grow when we acknowledge our failings.

The biggest danger for a procrastinator is when there is no time frame allocated to a task. This is usually the case in life. If there is no time deadline, then there is a likelihood that the task will continually be delayed. Have you ever said, "One day I will..." — insert task. Chances are this task was never completed. Or have you ever heard the goal, "I want to get fit?" This is a perfect example of a vague goal without a time frame. No wonder people aren't getting fit! We keep delaying a task through procrastination because there is no deadline. Procrastinators generally meet deadlines (even with low quality work) so long as there is a deadline.

Time is the procrastinator's biggest enemy but also the biggest ally if used correctly. From a motivation perspective, there isn't much more motivating than having very little time left to accomplish a task.

A lot of the time, we think we are lazy or unmotivated when in reality, we just don't prioritize the task highly enough. If your life, or the life of someone you loved, relied on you to complete a task, you would probably run through fire to get that task done.

There is an island in the middle of the Pacific Ocean on the ring of Fire called Tofua. It is where my name and family originate from. It's an imposing place with an active volcano and almost nowhere for a boat to land. The seas around it are rough and dangerous, and the volcano towers into the sky. There is an ancient Polynesian saying, "Manako maka fai ki Tofua," literally translating to: *If you want valuable rocks, then you will need to find them in Tofua*. The rocks they refer to are special volcanic rocks highly prized for use in an underground oven called an umu or to decorate grave sites. They hold their heat like no other rock in Polynesia. The saying translates to: *The most valuable of goals in life require us to travel to the most difficult places*. So if you want something of value, you will need to travel to where the seas are rough and the mountains high. But once you meet those goals, then you will have them for life.

Pita Taufatofua

"The most valuable stones are found in the hardest to reach places". Looking out to Kao from the volcano of Tofua.

We were returning one day from a boat trip to Tofua. The seas were rough, and there were twelve of us on a small boat built for four. This was common when travelling in Tonga. On top of this, we had many sacks of volcanic stones to take back to our family graveyard to decorate my grandmother's grave. Sitting on the front of the boat holding onto the anchor chain was a guy we called Pier. We didn't know his real name, but he had a French legionnaire's hat; so Pier it was. The sides of the boat were only inches above the waterline from the weight of the load. Within minutes of leaving the island, a huge wave crashed over us. Pier was washed right over into the ocean, while still holding that anchor chain. The captain slowed down the boat, and we all pulled Pier, with his stunned look, back on board.

Why is this story important? You will soon see. If I asked you to sit in a bathtub of water with a bucket and empty it out, you would probably be able to. Now, if I told you to sit in a bathtub for twelve hours and continually empty the tub as more water came in, you would fight and refuse the task. After Pier washed overboard, my father and I sat inside the boat with buckets and bailed water over the side for twelve hours straight, all while each subsequent wave would bring more water into the boat. The trip was meant to be a four-hour journey, but the seas were so rough that we had to slow right down while two of us bailed water to prevent being swamped by the waves and thus drowning.

When the price you pay for not doing a task isn't high in your priority scale, then you can find excuses not to do the task. Not emptying water from a bathtub for twelve hours has no consequence, and so you don't do it. Not bailing water from the boat that day would have meant drowning; we did it without a second thought. The price of not doing it was too high. By making the consequences of not doing a task seem more immediate we can bypass our task avoidance or procrastination processes. If we think of our long-term success and happiness the same way we think of our short-term impulses, then we will live a life of ambition.

The underlying emotion to procrastination is that the pain of doing the task now is greater than the joy you get at a later date for accomplishing that task. This leads to the task being left until later. People who haven't trained their self-discipline want what is easy right now, i.e. doing nothing or doing something unrelated to what needs to be done. As the deadline to a task draws closer, if the task is not completed, the delayed joy of completing the task becomes "immediate anxiety causing pain." So the procrastinator gets the task done. They must do this because if they don't, what was once delayed pain becomes immediate pain. Fear of pain is one of the strongest motivators.

Have you ever heard someone say that they do their best work under pressure? The truth of the matter isn't that they do their best work; it is that they become relatively more productive because they have no choice but to be. If they don't get it done, then they experience pain. Many of you and I will perform really well under pressure, and there will be those of you who struggle and crumble with pressure. Just because I perform well under pressure doesn't mean that I should leave things until the last minute or avoid them completely. This thinking will rob you of life and ability to finish high-quality tasks. You will be running at a level of mediocre. You're not put on this planet to be mediocre!

Procrastination is rarely an energy expenditure problem as much as it is a time priority problem. You may have an assignment or important paper due next week but end up spending a whole day doing smaller priority tasks like washing a car. After all, in our mind at least we are still achieving something, so we can justify away the important task. From an energy expenditure perspective, we may actually use more energy to complete the procrastination task over the important task. Why do we do this? Well for starters humans don't like doing what they're obligated to do as opposed to what they want to do. We would much rather clean the car because we don't have to than finish our assignment because we need to. It's a form of oppositional defiance, which means we do what we want. Well at least until the pain of a negative outcome from not doing the primary task gets too strong, i.e. our deadline.

If deadlines help us achieve something, couldn't we then circumvent our avoidance of a task by creating deadlines? We absolutely can! This is one of the main reasons that when we are taught to set a goal, we are also taught to give a date for which the goal must be accomplished. Sometimes this date is arbitrary or random and sometimes it is aligned with an external date such as was in my case, to qualify for an Olympic Games.

When I made the decision to try for a Winter Olympic Games, I did so very publicly. By telling the World that I would attempt to qualify for a second Olympics in under a year in a new sport, I, in essence, created a high-pressure deadline. This deadline could not be moved because it had a set date that was out of my control for the Winter Olympics. It was me that had to do what was required to qualify in such a short space of time. Deadline pressure along with making it public meant I had no choice but to complete the task or die trying so to speak. There was no backing out. And exactly one year later on the last race of the last qualification day, I managed to qualify for my first Winter Olympics with less than twelve weeks on skis. This was after close to ten failed races. The power of a time constraint works miracles to achieving goals. This doesn't mean that you have to announce your goals to the world. That is entirely up to you. What it does mean is that you need always to have a deadline, a line in the sand that must be met.

There are two ways to create deadlines.

1) Arbitrary False-time Deadline

This is a very powerful tool. The way it works is that we create a deadline for a specific task to be done by. If the task is small, such as to clean the kitchen, then we may set a timer for twenty-five minutes. An element of our subconscious knows that there is a timer running in the background and so we work to beat it. It becomes more of a game and a competitive challenge. The amount of time we set depends on the person. Whilst I like to set no more than twenty-five minutes for most tasks, this may be too short or too long for others. Find what works for you; do that for a larger task such as getting fit. We could choose a date or an event to get fit for. By assigning a specific deadline, we are now much more motivated to meet this deadline. We can even hold ourselves accountable by letting friends or family or the World know what it is that we are doing. Again, this step is up to you. Some people have the discipline to create these deadlines and goals without anyone ever knowing.

2) Pre-set Deadline

A pre-set deadline is one that you have no control over. This may be the date a paper is due or an event is held. Pre-set deadlines work well for procrastinators so long as they are able also to create smaller sub-deadlines. The purpose of the sub deadline is to break the task up into smaller pieces to complete along the way so that they're not left with a mammoth task at the end. Later in the book, I talk more on breaking the task into smaller parts. But for now, just know that if you constantly avoid doing the task, then it is too big for your current level of self-discipline, break it down smaller, it really is that simple.

To beat our procrastination habit, we must give ourselves deadlines for tasks. The reason we are not doing a task or delaying it is that we feel that we don't need to complete it there and then. Well, that's what we tell our self. If you find yourself procrastinating, you will also find that the task is just too overwhelming. Step 8 in the motivation guide will help you break that task into smaller sub-tasks. Our goal, just like beating laziness, is to move and do something no matter how small towards the goal we are wanting to achieve. Remember that procrastination robs you of time. Time is our strongest currency; we have a limited amount of it in our life. Don't let procrastination rob you of life.

The Comfort Zone

"Man is made to move and to grow. The comfort zone should only be a place of rest, not of living."

Goal — In this chapter, you will try to recognize the comfort zones that exist in your life. We will look at how they formed and why you need to be constantly growing and progressing in life.

The comfort zone is where most of us live, it is where we are comfortable. A better word for it would be a familiarity zone. After all, comfort has positive connotations whereas familiarity is more neutral and describes it better. It is a place which we know and understand. It could be the job you've been in for the last ten years. It could be the small house that you currently live in or the level of income that you have been receiving. It could be the routines that make up your day or even the toxic relationships that you settle for. The problem with comfort zones isn't that they are comfortable, it is that they don't allow growth. Humans are made to move and to grow. The comfort zone should only be a place of rest, not of living. Let me say that again. The comfort zone should only be a place of rest, not of living. We should always be aspiring to do better and to do more in life. This ties in with your purpose. Remember our purpose isn't small, it is a grand masterpiece that needs us to express it.

If it was possible to sit down all day and do nothing whilst still being happy and feeling fulfilled, then that is what many of us would do. The problem is that there is a little voice in our head that always wants more, and we deserve more. It isn't a bad thing always wanting more. It is only bad if that search for more requires you to do things that negatively affect your morals and principles or the lives of others. Wanting more isn't just about material growth but spiritual, physical and mental growth. We need to be growing in all areas of our life. When we stop growing, we open ourselves up to feelings of depression, negative thought, and we can become dissatisfied with life. Remember the kid who follows the butterfly with curiosity, that is how we need to grow. The happiness isn't in catching the butterfly but in chasing after it.

As I mentioned earlier, a comfort zone could be a toxic relationship. Not necessarily a comfortable thing to be in, but if all someone has ever known are toxic relationships, then that is where they may find themselves over and over. I have worked with many people both in the homeless shelters and in sports who weren't even aware that they were living in toxic comfort zones. I have seen examples of this not only in troubled youth but also in trained professionals. How is it that someone who is trained in dealing with people's problems couldn't deal with their own? Simple, it's easier and requires less work and pain to deal with other people's issues than it is our own. Whilst something may be as clear as day to an onlooker, more often than not, we aren't aware of our own comfort zone or habits of familiarity even when they result in a negative outcome for us.

The longer someone has lived in a comfort zone, the harder it becomes to move out of that zone. There is a timeless saying, "You can't teach an old dog new tricks." Or said another way, it is extremely difficult to teach someone new habits or how to move out of their comfort zone — challenging, but certainly achievable.

The longer you have been in a comfort zone, the more work you will have to apply to break out of it. I have been in many comfort zones throughout my life. Some in sport, some in finance and some in relationships. I have had periods where I felt that my training wasn't progressing. I was putting in the hours but wasn't getting the results. When I look back through those periods, I thought that the solution was to work harder. I would go to more training sessions and push myself to even higher levels of stress and pain. And still no progress. I was in a training plateau. The way out of a plateau isn't just to work harder but to work smarter. For twelve years, I had missed out on Olympic qualification, a long comfort zone to be sitting in. This may sound like an extreme comfort zone for some, but for me, it certainly was a comfort zone, as minimal training growth was happening within it. Because I had little progress, I must have been repeating the same things over and over, expecting a different outcome. It was a training comfort zone. And because I had been there so long, it meant I required even higher levels of hard and smart work to break out of it.

So what did I do? I went back to basics. I broke down the thoughts that were going on in my head during every session, and I used a form of the *raging wolf technique* to change them. You will learn more about this technique in the following chapters. Basically, it is a technique you use to change one thought that doesn't help you into another that does. I changed up everything training wise. I decided to train smarter and directed all of my focus to incremental improvements.

My goal became, to improve a small amount say 1% each session. Instead of just kicking pads and bags I would aim to improve an area of my technique with every strike. No training session was done without a goal for improvement within it. I was no longer going through the motions, but targeting progress, I started to work smarter, making tiny amounts of progress. They all added up to results. If you find that you are spinning the wheels in certain areas of your life and achieving the same results, then chances are you are in a comfort zone. Just because you want to break free from it doesn't mean it will happen. But it is the first step.

So how do we break free of a comfort zone? And how do we get motivated enough to do so? The secret to breaking through from a comfort zone to an area of growth requires the same elements that go into a nuclear fission reactor. For those who don't know how nuclear fission works the simple version is that we get a small amount of radioactive material and fire neutrons at it. When that neutron hits the material, the atom's chemical bonds break apart and cause huge amounts of stored energy to be released. A small amount of targeted material can create an enormous amount of energy. To break out of our comfort zone, we need to add a targeted amount of energy into the area that we are stuck in. Only once we pay the price and apply that neutron can we level up into our next level of growth. The price we pay is work and extreme focus. It is a price you will have to pay every single day until it becomes seamless. You will need to break down all the small habits that you engage in within your comfort zone. If you are at a certain weight you will need to look at your diet, exercise, and sleep plan, you will have to go back to basics. If your financial situation needs growth, you will need to be honest with yourself about your spending, saving, and money-making habits. Change and growth aren't free.

It isn't just hard work that we must apply to jump out of our comfort zone but focused smart work. We can't hit radioactive material with a hammer and expect large amounts of energy to be released. This is the equivalent of just working hard and not smart. And so hard work while crucial isn't enough. We need targeted hard work. Practice doesn't make perfect, but perfect practice makes perfect. Read that last line again. Practice doesn't make perfect but perfect practice makes perfect.

Are there areas of your life that have remained stagnant? Are there areas where you would like to progress? I cannot stress enough that you will have to do work to move to the next level. Sometimes we stay in our comfort zone because, quite simply, people just don't want to put in the work required. Once you have made peace with the fact that you will need to work and get *uncomfortable*, you will start growing as a person; you will start moving towards your big purpose. This will be a time of excitement where what you are doing is aligned with who you know you are becoming.

One of my greatest strengths is being able to embrace discomfort. Whether in training or in life, my comfort zone is so broad that what I find comfortable, many would find uncomfortable. This lets me get those extra few reps in at the gym or sleep like a baby whether in a tent or in a five-star hotel. Practice being uncomfortable in situations by slowly introducing these situations into your life. If you are uncomfortable talking in front of people, start by having a conversation with the cashier at the grocery store. If your comfort zone is always needing to be around people, schedule a day or a week just being in your own company. If you're stuck in a job you hate, then find ways to practice living with less money until you can find a job you love. This doesn't mean quitting your job, but it does mean training yourself to experience discomfort until you have the strength to take a leap into the amount of discomfort needed to grow. It is the last and hardest repetitions with a set of weights that give you the most growth in life.

Find little things within your comfort zone that you can incrementally improve. Make the improvements so small that you ease yourself into discomfort. For some, you will be able to take bigger steps into an area that makes you uncomfortable because you have already trained yourself to know that just because something is uncomfortable, it doesn't mean that it is bad for you. These days I embrace being uncomfortable, so much so that very little phases me. The irony is that this place of discomfort is in a way comfortable and so I am satisfied and happy whilst still being able to grow. This only comes through practice. Start small, and you will find that the more you become okay with being uncomfortable, the quicker you will grow and the happier and less afraid you will become.

Pita Taufatofua

Remove Negative People

"The only person living your life is you. Anyone who attacks your positive mindset doesn't deserve a spot in your day."

Goal — The goal of this chapter is to help you identify the people who take away goodness and positivity from your life. We look at why they do it and stress the importance of removing them from your day to day experience.

Every kid on my island dreamed of their first day in high school. With the new people, the new opportunities, the sports, a chance to grow up and have more freedom, it was an exciting time. My first day at high school, I was hit across the lower back into submission by a teacher with a two by four piece of wood. A handful of friends and I were excited to be coming back together after a long holiday. We couldn't find our classroom as the school in Tonga was new to us. A large male teacher with tree trunk arms saw us walking around the school and accused us of avoiding class. He called us over to the school assembly area and lined us up. There was a large wooden chair nearby, and so he ripped the chair leg off from the seat. Then he proceeded to beat us in front of everyone, the students and teachers alike. It's a strange thing — being beaten on your first day at high school. If I cried, I would look weak in front of the other kids. If I acted tough, the teacher would keep beating me until I broke.

The Motivation Station

I had to find the balance of not falling from the blows whilst also not crying. We survived the beating and hobbled off around the building to cry where no one could see us. We quietly swore to each other about the teacher, making sure that he couldn't hear us. I eventually stumbled to my new classroom feeling angry and hurt. I walked in and sitting at the front of the class was my new form teacher, the same teacher who had just beaten me. High school wasn't looking fun.

To make matters worse, the eighth-grade bully who was much older and bigger than the rest of us would sit in the seat right in front of me. I was much smaller than the other kids. Confronting and fighting with the bigger boys helped me cope and fit in. It wasn't that I wanted to fight, but sometimes I felt that I had to. My father is dark skinned and Tongan, and my mother is white. One day the class bully, twice my size, turned to me in class and said that my mother should go back to her country as people like her were stealing and didn't belong in Tonga. She was a nurse, and we were very poor. Furious, I stood up and broke my chair over the bully's back, this resulted in a brawl. We both ended up in the Principals office crying and asking each other for forgiveness. We didn't want our parents to find out we fought in school as that meant more punishment. So we hugged and told the principal we were best buddies; our parents never found out. Growing up in Tonga was a strange mix of fighting and forgiving.

I couldn't choose who my classmates or teacher would be, and so for two years, I was forced to find a way to deal with the anger from being beaten without triggering more fights or beatings. It wasn't that the teacher wanted to beat me specifically as he hit everyone. It was more that something in his life was causing unresolved pain, and he couldn't handle his anger. I pretended to do what I was told when he was around and eventually ended up with good grades. Had I not been young and dependent, I could have been stricter on choosing the people around me. In this case, I would have to weather the storm, and I did, and I learned very quickly how to survive high school.

I don't know if some form of karma ever found my teacher for beating us. Maybe it did, and maybe it didn't. What I can say is that many years later, I found myself standing behind him waiting in line for food at a cafe. He looked at me, smiled, and shook my hand. I looked him straight in the eyes, and I smiled back. I had no hate. Holding on to any pain he had caused would have been like imprisoning myself in my own mind. What he did wasn't right, but letting it go gave me freedom to not live in the past. I didn't want him to experience the pain he gave us. If so, then I would have been no different from him, perpetuating a cycle of pain. Forgiveness can really be liberating.

There are not many more de-motivating influences than negative people. Just as you find yourself in a good routine kicking goals, someone says something that takes all the wind out of your sails. It could be a small comment or backhanded remark that unravels weeks or months of work. Imagine spending months in the gym losing weight. You are happy with your progress. When out of nowhere someone who you may or may not know says something that makes you feel bad. A negative comment. Regardless of your mindset before the comment, you are now in a negative space about your goals.

Being strong is about being resilient to negativity. Nothing should affect you. But until you reach that level of strength, it is extremely important to minimize your exposure to negative people. Even the strongest of us can only lift so much weight. This is a two-fold process, building resilience to negativity and removing negativity.

My life has been a somewhat interesting mixture of positive and negative influences. Whilst I have been blessed with a supportive family, the vast majority of people I have been exposed to did not believe in me or in my capability to achieve great things, let alone anything. To give it an arbitrary number, I would say that 5% of people I knew believed in my ability to become successful, and 95% did not. The challenges came when that 95% included my friends or a partner. One of the most soul-crushing things is when people you care deeply for do not believe in your capability to succeed. Some of the most significant milestones in my life were when there was a relationship breakup because a partner didn't believe in the vision that I would one day become an Olympian or one day be successful. They saw the now, not *the soon*. This is how life is. Sometimes, it is your inability to communicate your capacity, and sometimes it is because the other person doesn't see as far as you can see.

Not everyone will see the dreams that you have, and that is okay. If you were to give it a number, what percentage of people in your life have been consistently supportive or consistently negative towards your dreams? Be honest with yourself and look at the language that they have used with you. Whilst you may think certain language is nothing more than a friendly joke, it all adds up, positive or negative. Sit back for a little and digest those numbers, they are part of the overall picture as to why you are who you are or why you do what you do. You become the people around you. That's a scary thought for a lot of us!

I have worked with clients who, I could safely say, have spent most of their life with nothing but negative people. I had positive family members, but many of my clients did not. In listening to some of the youth, I heard that they had never had a single person tell them just how proud they were of them. Or that they could achieve anything they put their mind to. Imagine that, going through your whole developmental life without someone telling you that you are capable or worthy or loved. We can start to see just why people are who they are. My mother told all of us kids when growing up that we could achieve anything we put our mind to, and still, to this day, we believe her. But not all of you reading this would have had these positive role models, and most of the young people I worked with didn't have any. The good news is that despite your circumstances or the people you had in your life growing up, you are capable of change. You are capable of choosing the person that you want to be and the people you want around you. And if you have never heard it, then I am proud of you and believe that you can achieve anything you set your mind to. You have made it this far into a book on motivation and self-development. That tells me already that your life is changing, and you are growing, and whilst these may look like words on a page, behind them is a message from me of appreciation and pride in just who you are becoming.

There are two types of people. Those who turn negativity into personal pain or those who use it as fuel for growth. I'm sure you've read countless stories about people, who despite the worst circumstances, found their way to success and happiness. These sorts of people used negative and demotivating comments to take on an "I'll show you" attitude.

When I was twelve years old, I took up playing rugby as a school sport in Tonga. For four years straight I trained every single day, never missing a training session. And for four years straight I was never once given a run on the rugby field. Not even a single minute in the dying moments of a game. I was physically smaller than all the other kids, and perhaps this is why my coaches never gave me a chance. Instead, I cut oranges and ran water out to the other kids, for four years. They were my friends, so I never once complained. I was happy seeing them play despite also wanting to have some game time myself. Being bitter about this was a possibility.

But instead of taking on a negative emotion I used it as fuel for my growth fire. Instead of allowing other people's perceptions of me dictate my future I created my own perception of myself. The kid who never got picked in the team went on to become a two-sport Olympian. It is completely up to us what we do with other people's criticisms. Do they burn you or do they fuel you? Chose fuel and your life will change for the better.

But what if we are in the first group of people who aren't in a position yet to take negativity and use it for fuel? The simple answer is that we must first reduce our access to negative people whilst we build our own internal resilience. The people you surround yourself with will have a massive impact on not only your levels of motivation but also your levels of happiness, choose them wisely.

To understand negative people, we must first understand what drives people. Do you have that friend, co-worker or family member who is constantly putting you down or saying negative things? No matter what you do, they find ways to criticize you? They could be someone as close as your parents or as distant as a stranger off the street. There are at least two people involved in every negative interaction. You and the negative influencer. In order for you to feel a negative emotion from a comment two things must happen. The negative influencer must say something negative, and you must accept or be affected by what they say. If we remove one or both of these conditions, you are no longer affected negatively.

The goal is to build internal strength where very little of what is said to you affects you. Until that happens, you should minimize your exposure to a negative influencer and their negativity. Be kind with how you do this to the person so as not to create animosity but be ruthless internally in your conviction to remove toxic people from your life.

The psychology of why people do things could be a topic for a whole new book. For the sake of quick, solid information this negative person has one or more of three major reasons as to why they attack or criticize you. These are control, fear, and personal self-esteem.

The Control Influencer

Control is generally used by people who you know as opposed to a stranger. By saying something negative about you, they, in their mind, get a feeling of power over you. They feel this way because your emotional state changes in response to whatever their comment

was. This power is intoxicating for some people. Almost like a drug, it says you are a slave to my comments, and thus I have power over you.

These people put others down as a way to bring themselves up, well, at least in their mind.

Sometimes this person is conscious of what they are doing, and sometimes they do it subconsciously. Often a narcissist will take you on an emotional roller coaster to further cement in this power. They will mix periods of negativity with glimpses of great loving times to further their control over you. By giving you glimpses of the good times, you live in a state of wanting this despite spending the most time in their negative control.

The controlling influencer, out of the three, is who you want to run from the fastest. They aren't ready to change, nor do they want to. They've gone through life using control as a means to get what they want, usually significance and power. The game with this kind of person is rigged in a way that you cannot win because it is, after all, their rules. The solution? Don't play the game. They aren't ready to be self-reflective enough to grow. Wish them the best and move on. Save your energy for your goals. Being controlling they will try even harder to put you down when you decide to leave, be ready for this. By leaving, you are taking the thing they value most, their control and in doing so you take back your personal power.

The Fearful Influencer

The fearful person says negative things to you because they are scared of change. You are a known quantity. By your growing and achieving your goals, you suddenly become an unknown quantity. Many people fear change. They are scared of seeing someone they care for become someone they don't completely understand, and so they work to sabotage that progress.

The motivating element for this person is that they feel scared of losing you. Or more specifically scared to lose the 'current' you. This person may say something like "you should get a real job" or "that's too difficult for you." They aren't particularly spiteful, but they are misguided. Fear should only be used as its original purpose, a survival mechanism. It's how we escaped from the jaws of animals or warring tribes. Not as a way of avoiding relative safe, uncertainty. These people are driven by fear of loss. They are scared to lose you.

True strength comes from being happy in seeing others progress and providing support if and when they fail. Sometimes the best way to approach the fearful influencer is through a loving conversation. By letting them know that you may change in certain ways but that you will always value and care for them along your journey can do wonders to how they then treat you. Using positive reinforcement when they say good things and defiance when they say negative things, you are training them in how they should treat you. People treat you the way you allow and teach them to treat you. Should they then step up their negativity and become like the controlling influencer, you must remove them from your daily sphere. Negativity in whatever form is demotivating and hindering to your success and happiness.

The Self-esteem Influencer

People say things, not as a reflection of the other person, but as a reflection about their inner self. Have you ever seen groups of people who all carry the same negative belief? People tend to gravitate to others who have similar beliefs both positive and negative. The goal of the self-esteem influencer is to say negative things to you in a way that justifies their own outlook on life. After all, misery loves company. Their self-esteem is tied to creating a bubble of people around them that share their thoughts and values. This helps them avoid the truth of their own personal decisions. After all, if everyone thinks the same thing, then it must be right — well, at least in their mind.

A great example of this could be seen in a family where many within the family struggle with food and weight challenges. How common is it to see a healthy, fit member within such a family? Not common at all. There will be some alpha member, normally a mother or father, who will unintentionally pass on their unhealthy thoughts about food choice to the other family members. If everyone around you struggles with this, then you can be assured that the language around food is geared to accepting poor eating habits. Unfortunately, research around health and physical wellbeing says that obesity is an epidemic, growing worldwide and leading to shorter life expectancy. The family leader may say something like "Well, you could get hit by a bus, might as well enjoy food while you're alive." Many may not want to see someone in their life fit and healthy because it is a constant reminder of their own choices with food. This makes them feel bad. It is easier to try and change you than it is to look inside and change themselves. Once you get to a stage of being fit and healthy and are able to influence them positively, their manner towards you will change. It is at this point that you can positively influence them toward changing their habits in a healthier direction.

An alcoholic is another example of a self-esteem influencer. I have never consumed drugs or an alcoholic drink. I went through my teens and twenties with many people, including partners, trying to convince me that I was missing out. There was very real pressure to conform. In my mind, life was great, and I was growing; I didn't need drugs or alcohol. Being a defiant young adult, I actually took up an oppositional stance to anyone trying to force their choices on me. Still to this day, I have lived drug and alcohol-free. This isn't to say that my choices are correct, but it says that they are correct for me, and your best self-choices will be correct for you. Never let anyone make you feel otherwise.

Getting back to the alcoholic, they may say something like "just have one drink" or "you're my drinking buddy." This is okay, so long as it is your informed choice and in moderation. But someone who values you will never put you in a position that questions your own values or health to justify their decisions and provide them with entertainment. Someone who consumes alcohol to excess and encourages you to do the same does so because it is more enjoyable for them. Your letting loose is a form of entertainment for them; it is not based on what's best for you unless it is your choice. Your drinking heavily makes them feel better about how much they drink. Always be aware of what someone's motivations are behind the advice they give you. They may not even be aware that their advice is based on their personal benefit over yours. Question everything and choose only that advice which will benefit your life.

Self-esteem influencers hold an extremely negative self-image which is tied strongly to other's opinions of them. Their self-talk is surface level as going any deeper is too painful. Their reasoning is that the more people they can get who support their negative ideals the more justified they are in their actions. In their mind, if everyone thinks a certain way, then that way must be correct. Nothing could be further from the truth.

Self-esteem influencers can be great people, but unless they are willing to provide you positive encouragement despite their own battles, then they too must not be in your daily bubble of people. Many people don't even realize that the advice they tend to give is tainted with bias towards an outcome that improves *their* experience as opposed to benefitting the person receiving that advice.

We should also note that at times we, ourselves, are the negative influencer with others. When we haven't gotten ourselves together, we can negatively impact those around us. Sometimes we don't see it, sometimes we do and don't know how best to address our behavior without losing the person we negatively influence. It's easy to call someone else a negative and toxic person and never address our own shortcomings. Ensure we measure ourselves with the same stick that we measure others. And if we find we fall short of that measurement, then it's time to remove ourselves from those we can hurt while we make the necessary changes to heal.

Removing negative people from your day to day life will have a profound effect on your motivation levels.

Negative people will either keep you stagnant or undermine all the progress that you make. Be very clear with people on your expectations of how you deserve to be treated. An *attempt* already has an element of failure-justification implied in it. Don't attempt to remove people who hurt you purposely. Remove yourself from them. Never settle for less than all the goodness you deserve. It is your life and whether you achieve your goals may very well depend on the people you allow into your life. As you build resilience to negativity, you will find yourself in a position where very little affects you, and everything becomes either positive or a lesson for growth.

Negative Thoughts and Depression

"Sometimes we have to fight for the happiness that we deserve. Once we learn how to do this, we set ourselves up for a future of joy by removing the fears that once controlled us."

Goal — The goal of this chapter is to talk about depressive, negative thoughts that hinder our growth and happiness. We then look at my favorite tools you can employ immediately to help deal with these negative ways of thinking. Please, if you, or your loved ones, have persistent or chronic negative or harmful thoughts on any of these topics, seek immediate professional help. Helplines and walk-in clinics are available to assist people worldwide.

If only motivation was just about a few tricks you could do to help you stay motivated, then life would be easy. The truth is that long term motivation and happiness requires you to remove negative thinking and deal with whatever trauma and baggage you may be carrying from your past. It could have been a massive injustice or pain that happened to you. It could be a past relationship or the loss of a loved one. Some of these things may have happened when you were young or recently. Some may be your fault, and some may be the fault of others. I find motivation easy because I've learned how to deal with negative thoughts very quickly before they can take hold in my mind. I've also put in a lot of work to heal and consolidate any baggage or trauma that happened to me. Unresolved trauma will leak into your life when you least expect it. You can't avoid it and expect happiness; you must go straight through it. Only then will it disappear.

This is a tough chapter but has some deep lessons. Grab some chocolate, a nice cup of tea and keep reading.

When I told people that I would be writing about depression and negative thinking in my motivation book they were scared. They were worried that different readers would have different reactions to the information I give. They thought it would be safer to avoid the issues than to risk the consequences of addressing them head-on. After pondering this for quite some time, I decided that a lot of the reason we go through life with baggage is that we avoid addressing things early on that can harm us in the long term. We tiptoe around our pain and fear and wonder why it controls us. Being an Olympian who has overcome great adversity, I believe that everyone has more strength than they realize. I decided that I would share some of the knowledge and tools that help me stay positive. Because of this, we will go headfirst into this chapter like the motivation warriors that we are.

We can't talk about motivation without also talking about depressive thinking and its effects on us. This way of thinking can lead to an extreme lack of motivation, and a lack of motivation can result in even more deep-rooted negativity. It's a vicious cycle. Not everyone reading this will suffer from depression, but most will experience moments in their life where they may to varying degrees. I am not a psychologist or a psychiatrist, but as a youth-worker working many years with homelessness, I have noticed common traits and witnessed many situations. I've seen both children and the strongest adults break down or come to a complete stop when everything appeared to be fine. I've mentored people who have been at the edge of self-sabotage or even worse, complete self-destruction. But I have also seen the most miraculous stories of everyday people overcoming adversity and successfully battling the demons of depression and negative thinking. I have seen so much hope and strength that I am excited to share what I now know.

Whether you have depressive thoughts or know someone who does, it is something that affects everyone at some stage. For many years I worked with people who suffered all levels of depression. When asking them what it felt like, there were some common themes. They said that there was a deep feeling of loneliness, sadness, and emptiness. There were feelings of pain and not being worthy or deserving of happiness. Sometimes the pain was just too much that they would stay in bed all day, or week or month or they would harm themselves. Motivation was secondary to survival and just getting through the day was a major accomplishment.

I saw that the depression demons don't sneak in the back door as fire breathing dragons; instead, they come through the front door as cunning, calm salesmen peddling their wares and whispering negativity in your ear. Those whispers would be ever so subtle, and as people allowed them to stay, they would grow and reveal their true destructive intentions. They weren't there to benefit your life but to hurt it.

One of the dangers with depressive thoughts is that they can make people so defensive that they are tricked into defending them. Barriers would go up, and advice and ideas would be met with resistance. Defending the 'right' to think negatively of oneself or of life is a slippery slope. When you start defending something that harms you, you are giving it permission to stay. By being nice to it, you assume it will be nicer to you.

Nothing could be further from the truth. I have always viewed depressive thoughts and negative thinking as a living, breathing thing that steals motivation and happiness from our life. While depression may have a strong hold on someone, it most certainly does not have the right to be there. You are the captain of your ship and the master of your destiny. The right you do have is to live a happy and fulfilled life. It can be scary thinking of depression as a living thing. But by seeing it alive and separate from us, we also learn that with help it can be overcome. We can assist in accomplish this by starving it of resources and destroying its goals as you will soon see. Continual progress is a weapon in our fight against self-negativity. Each step forward however large or small is a step towards a happier life, one that you deserve.

There are many forms of depression including temporary or chronic. From my experience working in shelters, I found some forms were environmental — nurture — and some likely had genetic factors — nature. And some were a mixture of the two. Environmental depression was based on external circumstances or triggers that influenced a person's mood or way of thinking. This could have been due to things that happened such as a troubled childhood or a relationship breakdown. They may have experienced huge financial losses or suffered an accident that triggered depression. Genetic aspects meant that some people were more prone to being depressed due to factors like serotonin regulation or pre-programmed thought patterns passed on through their family history.

Whatever the cause or how seemingly complex it appeared, there were certain tools that I found which could help an individual get lasting outcomes. These tools were some of many they could use in their battle through depressive thinking.

In the following chapters, we look at diet, exercise, and meditation. These along with prescribed medication are also tools to help in the fight against negative thoughts. A healthy and balanced body helps to combat depressive thoughts. Another tool that we have already addressed is removing toxic people from our lives. The goal here is to place ourselves in a positive and nurturing environment as much as possible. After that, it is up to us to do the work needed. It will be uncomfortable at times, and the volume of work will be high. But the trade-off will be well worth it. A lifetime of happiness.

I have seen over my years of work even the most complex and self-destructive of people pull themselves from the struggle of negative thinking and into a life of joy. Each person's toolbox to deal with depressive thoughts is different. Things that may help some people may be less effective on others. I have found certain tools that could be very effective and useful to add to your toolbox. And remember we all have the right to happiness and peace and a fulfilled life.

These four tools are:

1. **The Candle of Hope** – The light in every person
2. **The Raging Wolf** – To remove negative thoughts and replace them with positive ones
3. **The Horse and Four Riders** – Removing the burdens of life, one by one
4. **That One Thing** – Letting go of that one thing that still hurts you

Before I explain these tools, we need to clarify that there are individuals who are highly motivated and successful but also highly depressed. We only need to look at certain celebrities, sports stars and wealthy executives who have made it big but then ended up depressed or in rehab or worse. All people are created equal when it comes to being susceptible to life's ups and downs. All people can feel both great joy and deep pain; we all have our different challenges.

Depressive thoughts don't differentiate between people. They can find anyone, and so we must be aware that there are tools in our arsenal to combat them. Living a truly motivated life means being motivated in all areas of life, not just some. To be rich or successful needs to be accompanied by happiness, that is the goal. That said, it is much greater to be poor and happy than to be rich and miserable.

* * *

Pita Taufatofua

The Candle of Hope

"Hope is knowing that we can create our own light in the darkest of times."

How do you motivate someone who is at such a low point in life that food has lost its flavor and a blue sky looks grey? The short answer is patience, understanding and hope. A hope that the depression will pass, and they will soon be enjoying the happiness that they deserve. Hope is our first tool because it allows us to take that first step in the right direction. When we can't see the light at the end of the tunnel, we must believe that within all of us is our own candle of hope, we just need to light it. And we have all the tools within us to do this. But first, let me tell you a story that starts sad and ends with hope.

I worked with a fifteen-year-old female who I will call Rachel. We never used their real names to preserve their confidentiality. When it came to depressive thoughts, Rachel had it all, and she had every reason. Her mother, a heavy drug user, exposed Rachel to all forms of abuse. Being homeless was safer for Rachel than where she lived. When she came to our homeless shelter, she was a shell of who she would become. Despite her mother no longer being in her life, she continued to express some of the negative habits she learned from her upbringing. She did things that were extremely dangerous to her physical and mental wellbeing; it was all she knew.

To make matters worse, more trouble piled up as her health had deteriorated after being diagnosed firstly with complex mental health issues and then with leukemia, a cancer of the blood. When I would try to talk with Rachel, I found her to be constantly on edge, easily triggered, and seemingly lacking emotion. I figured out that her lack of emotion was a survival mechanism she had created to blunt the pain and trauma that she had gone through. One evening at three a.m., I received a call from a police officer that Rachel was standing on a bridge, holding on to the rail by one hand, and leaning over the edge. Police cars had shut off the bridge, and Rachel had asked to talk to me. Over the phone, she told me about how unfair her life was and asked why all these things had to happen to her. In that moment, I felt an overwhelming sense of empathy. She was right. Why did all these things have to happen to someone completely undeserving of all the pain? Why could life be so unfair?

From years of training, I calmly sympathized, telling her that she had every right to feel the way she felt, and that I didn't know why all these things happened. I told her that I would like to pick her up from the bridge and take her for a coffee so that we could try and unravel why life was that way for her. I told her that she was the captain of her own ship, and all choices in her life were hers.

It turns out that those words made a huge difference to Rachel. She later told me that it was the first time she knew that she could make her own choices without an adult dictating her life to her. She climbed back over the guard rail. This is when I truly learned that despite someone's history, having them know that they are the captain of their own ship and master of their destination is a powerful thing.

Rachel's story doesn't end there. She had many more ups and downs emotionally, and through our work with her she signed herself up to a six-month training course in an area she was interested in, photography. Throughout those months, we spoke a lot about what she would do with her new photography skills, all the countries she would visit and all the great experiences she would have. Slowly her focus started to change. The seed of hope was starting to grow, and her candle was beginning to light. She became less focused on all that had happened to her and more focused on what she would do, and all that was ahead of her. Her purpose was becoming greater than her problems.

One day she walked into the office with her new diploma of photography looking confused. I asked her what was wrong, she said she didn't know what to do with it. When I noticed that it was her diploma, I told her how proud I was of her accomplishing something all on her own and how we would all celebrate her achievement. I knew that in her mind she believed that she had never achieved anything and thus had never had a celebration of her success. She proudly put that diploma up on her wall.

Rachel went on to live independently, work through a university degree and last I heard she was in Cambodia working in an orphanage. Instead of focusing entirely on how unfair life could be she found her hope and her purpose.

Rachel's story is very powerful because from it I was able to use her experiences and lessons to reach even more people. She was one of my teachers in just how strong a person can be. Whether you are a Rachel, or you know a Rachel, remember to be kind to yourself and others because we never know what someone has gone through and yet we are all deserving of kindness. But we also learn what someone is capable of overcoming, once they see that the light, they seek is within them and that light is hope.

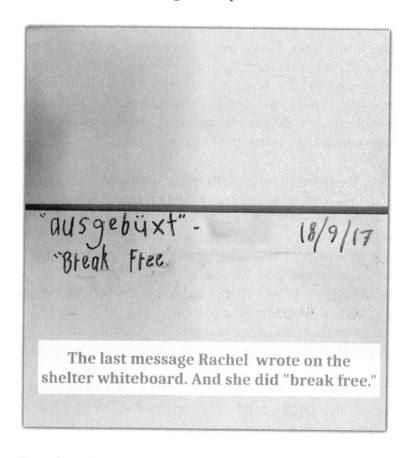

The last message Rachel wrote on the shelter whiteboard. And she did "break free."

Some key elements come out of Rachel's story. First was the understanding that life is rarely fair, and that once we could move past this, we could start to grow out of our negative thinking. Secondly was that despite the most terrible experiences happening to someone, they could come out on top should they be willing to put in the work. For people suffering from depression, it is powerful to know that time heals if you make that decision to put in the work. How long that time takes depends on how much work you are willing to put in.

The third was that each person is ultimately the captain of their own ship. Many of the storms and challenges that have happened in their life are not their fault and will pass. How their life turns out will depend on how they decide to steer their life forward and not focus on what was behind them. Searching for even the tiniest amount of Hope in the darkest of times will help you through any storm.

If you can't find joy when life feels dark, remember Rachel's story. Within each of us is a candle, a candle of hope. We light it by first recognizing we have it, and then by understanding that everything travels in seasons. Even the coldest winter will pass if we are prepared to light that candle. And once we know that we can generate the heat and light from within us, even our darkest days can become our brightest memories.

***

The Raging Wolf

"To remove negative thoughts and replace them with positive ones."

In my mind, negative thoughts have no power and rarely attempt to affect me. I have hit rock bottom numerous times. I have been completely broke, had relationships breakdown, suffered major career changing injury and watched friends and family members pass away. After I missed out on my first Olympic games, I spent three months in a wheelchair and another six on crutches. I slept in the basement of my mother's house as I couldn't walk or work. My relationship at the time was coming to an end as this beacon of martial arts strength was crippled and reliant on others.

On top of that, my Aunty Luisa who I was very close to passed away unexpectedly. She was an amazing and strong woman, who never complained and worked very hard. None of us knew how sick she was; she told no one right up till her final days.

I had two jobs, one as a youth worker and one working with a team in the finance sector. On the same day during the economic crisis, both companies went bust. I got two calls on one day that there was no longer a company to work for, and I would be out of work.

On that day, I had rented a small vessel to take a sixteen-year-old boy fishing whom I worked with at the shelter. He was diagnosed with having autism and would hyper-focus on activities he enjoyed. He lived for fishing and had spent the whole week preparing for our trip. While out in the river, the youth-care company called to say that all employees were redundant, their doors were closing, and to return the young person back home immediately. There were no longer funds to look after him. It was a tough blow. I felt the pain that my six years of dedicated work there was ending. But I felt even worse for the young boy, who had only just gotten bait onto his fishing line and was ready to cast. He would no longer have a home providing the care he required. I decided to stay out fishing with him all day. He had a blast. Upon returning the boat and walking to the car, I got the next ill-fated phone call. The owner of my second place of work had been charged with dodgy finance dealings while overseas and was sitting in a US jail awaiting trial. The company would be going under, and again, we were all being laid off. What a day. In the

spirit of my Polynesian mindset, I drove the boy to another fishing spot, and we sat there fishing for most of the night. He couldn't believe his luck, while I sat there scratching my head wondering what the hell had just happened.

It would be very easy to fall into depressive thoughts when everything is going wrong. I spent months at rock bottom. And what I learned was that it wasn't as scary as it appeared to be. Conditions and circumstances were out of my control, and those I left to the wind. Physically, I could hardly move after a bad knee injury, all I had was my mind. This is where a lot of my self-work started.

Being an engineer by study, I was obsessed with finding answers to problems. I would lay there and count how many times a particular negative thought would come into my head through the course of a day. I would time how long it would stay, and I would create metrics to understand what was happening in my brain. In those months I lay in that basement room, I studied everything I could find on how our brain works. I became obsessed with seeking knowledge. I listened to talks from some of the best inspirational speakers, and I started to break down my own psychology. Since those days in late 2007, I became impervious to negative thought. I calloused my brain and put in the work needed to strengthen my way of thinking. And in those days, I started developing one of my most effective tools, the raging wolf. This tool has been one of my strongest weapons against negative thought. It is an immediate barrier that goes up and prevents me ever dwelling in negativity. It is a tool that anyone can use, and it is extremely simple, as you will soon see.

I was talking to a young adult who had been kicked out of his last few jobs for lashing out violently at people. We were standing in a room at the homeless shelter playing pool, when I asked him what was going on in his life. He said that he always felt depressed, and that he couldn't escape the negative thoughts when he was alone. By lashing out and attacking people, he felt that he had some form of power. I stood back listening to him, and then I slammed the door to the pool room shut. I did it to shock him and to get his mind racing. I wanted him alert to the lesson I was about to give him in negative thinking. He was startled, and I still laugh when I remember the look on his face when I slammed that door. I asked him what would happen if a raging wolf stuck its head into the room and bit him. What would he feel? He said he would feel pain, anger and maybe a little bit of fear.

I then asked him, if after being bitten by the wolf, whether he would reach down and gently pat it and feed it, or would he be more inclined to flick it on the nose? He said he would prefer to flick the wolf on the nose and slam the door shut on it. The idea of a slamming door was fresh in his brain. I said, "How would you train the wolf not to want to attack you"? He said he would keep flicking its nose until it learned that it wasn't welcome in the room, and that it would feel pain every time it tried to bite him. I said, "Now imagine that this room is your mind, and that the raging wolf is a negative thought." He looked at me with a stunned light-bulb moment look. And so, meet the raging wolf, the negative thought that attacks us when we least expect it.

The idea of a technique to deal with a raging wolf came to me from a Native American story. In it a strong and wise warrior is sitting around a campfire talking to his grandson. The warrior tells the grandson that within all of us there is a fierce battle between two wolves. The first is the Wolf of Evil, who represents pain and fear, sorrow, jealousy, and all negative thoughts. The second is the Wolf of Good, who represents joy, peace, happiness, and positive thoughts. The grandson then asks the warrior which wolf wins? The grandfather replies, "The one that you feed."

Why is it that we can easily understand something in the physical space, and how we should approach a raging wolf, but we struggle to do the same in our mind? The truth is that the way we solve a problem in the physical world also applies to how we can address certain problems in our mind. If we think of a depressive or negative thought as the raging wolf, then it makes no sense to feed it and pat it every time it bites us. We don't want it in our lives. But that is exactly what we do. We try to placate or appease the raging wolf. We experience a negative thought, and instead of flicking it in the nose and slamming the door the second it arrives, we sit there with it, and dwell on it and look at it from a thousand different angles.

By doing this, we teach the raging wolf or negative thought that biting us and causing pain is okay, and that it will be rewarded. When something gets rewarded, it continues to stay and associates its pain-causing behavior with a reward. We must think of depressive, negative thoughts as living, breathing things. I mean, if they weren't living, then they would be like an inanimate object, i.e. a rock or table or chair, none of which can cause us pain by themselves. But they continue to cause us pain and therefore must have a life of their own. The benefit of them being alive is that we recognize that they aren't us, and that like all living things that try to attack us, they can be trained or removed or hurt back. Yes, it is possible that we can hurt a negative thought to the point where it will bite us less and less and eventually stop if we bite back.

The way to remove or train a negative thought is to flick it on the nose the second it arrives. We must become aware that we are having a negative thought, and the moment we are aware, we do something to swap out that thought. This normally starts with movement and then flooding your mind with positive words. If for example, I had a negative thought come into my mind telling me how bad my life was and how unworthy I was of love or happiness, I would start the process by first acknowledging that I am having that thought. I would then quickly stand up and move, this could be a five-minute walk or ten squats — any movement. Moving the body changes the chemistry of the mind. As I would do this, I would say out loud all the things that were positive in my life. If you feel depressed, you may believe this list is small; it isn't. But prepare it in advance for when those thoughts come. You will do this as often as you can to the point where it becomes more painful to entertain a negative thought message than a positive one, and you will burn some calories in the process, while releasing your happy chemical, endorphin; what a win.

The raging wolf technique works by causing pain to the negative thought. It then re-associates a trigger that would normally cause negative thoughts with a positive outcome. What happens when you train your mind enough times to do this? You've got it; it begins to rewire the same way it rewires when you learn skills through repetition. The longer you've been entertaining negative thoughts, the more work and self-discipline you will have to apply to overcome them. But like all things the harder and smarter you work, the greater the reward and the quicker you arrive there.

Next time that negative thought decides to enter your mind, take immediate action and move. Flood the mind with positive thoughts. Do this often enough, and you will find that you will start to think differently and more positively. The doors of your mind will automatically shut on the raging wolf.

Any negative triggers won't result in hours of self-loathing but in moments of positive thinking.

* * *

The Horse and Four Riders

"Removing the burdens of life, one by one."

Depression is overwhelming. The more things we have in our life that are going wrong, the harder it becomes to do anything, let alone be motivated. We become weighed down by the burden of multiple problems. When we have multiple problems, motivation suffers as we move into survival mode.

When I was a young boy growing up in Tonga, we had a horse. As kids, we use to ride that horse to the farm as a means of transport. Because we could only afford one horse, it was common for myself and three cousins to all ride it at the same time. The horse would struggle under the load but would always somehow get us to the farm so that we could harvest the sweet potato we would eat. The problem came when one warm summer's day we decided to try and cross a reef joining two islands. The island on the other side had the most beautiful sandy beaches but was only accessible during low tide when the reef could be crossed by horse. In those days we couldn't afford a boat. At high tide, the water was too deep, and many people who had attempted to make that crossing were washed away and never seen again. We slowly approached the reef all four of us sitting on that poor horse. After about fifty meters in, the horse just wouldn't budge. The weight of all four riders mixed with the increasing current was just too much for the horses' present strength. We were stuck on a reef unable to move.

The horse and all four riders had completely come to a standstill. It was doing its best just to stand there and not collapse under the pressure of the incoming tide. Very similar to us when burdens of the world try to weigh us down. After some clever problem solving, we decided that two of us would find a piece of the reef that we could stand on while the other two rode the horse to the far side. One person would then return on the horse and pick up the next person off the reef and so forth until we were all on the beautiful shores of our favorite beach. Our goal was to get across safely, and the only way the horse was going to do that was to remove the load and do it one person at a time. One of three things needed to change for us to get across to the beautiful beach. Either the horse needed more strength, less load to carry or the tidal current needed to subside. Training the horse to be stronger was an option, but that would require time, time we didn't have. We had no control over the current or the tides. But what we could do was remove the burden of weight one by one until the task was completed.

Depression and negative thoughts are made worse when there are compounding problems. Like a horse with four riders, you can find yourself stuck and unable to move towards your goals. If you are having relationship issues, financial problems, difficulties at work, and all at the same time, then the burden may be just too much for you to overcome. Like the horse on the reef, you find yourself stuck and unable to move. Your goal becomes survival. To move through that feeling of being overwhelmed, you should approach each of those problems one at a time. Trying to tackle them all at once is like trying to ask the horse to carry all four people across that reef. At some point, it will be too much and may end up washed away by the current.

Be okay with parking a problem while you deal with another. This is the smart way to approach challenges. Parking a problem doesn't mean you won't address it; it just means you will address it at a later stage when you are capable of doing so.

So which challenge should you work on first? There is no right or wrong answer. Normally I would say work on the problem that is most pressing. What I mean by this is the problem that the consequences of not completing it are the greatest. If you're having financial difficulties and can't pay your rent, preventing yourself from becoming homeless is probably a higher priority than, say, your goal of losing ten pounds. In this case, you would park your weight-loss goal temporarily while focusing in on working for a stable income. Once your income is relatively stable, you can turn your focus to the next challenge. By giving 100% focus to each problem, you alleviate the overwhelming nature of addressing all the problems at once. You also acknowledge that you will get around to dealing with each challenge, just one at a time. You aren't getting rid of all your challenges; you are simply temporarily parking them with the intent that you will get back to them as your strength increases or as your other more pressing problems decrease in number. Once you are capable, you may even have the strength to address more than one challenge at a time. This will come as you build your resilience muscle.

This step isn't about curing depressive thoughts. It is about removing things that add to the challenges someone is already facing. The less weight on our shoulders, the less pain we feel and the more focused we become to address our challenges one at a time.

* * *

Let Go of that One Thing

"Letting go of that thing that hurts you the most will give you freedom."

Everyone has that one thing. That thing they think about way too often. The thought or trauma that often causes them the most pain, and that takes away the majority of their thinking time. They stress and stew over it. It could be a relationship problem or something that happened to them as a child. It could be something that someone said to them years ago, and that still affects them to this day or pain or injustice that someone caused them. It could be a fear about the future or what will happen to them or a loved one at a later date. Whatever it is, it continues to weigh you down and take up way too much of your precious focus. It's time to let it go.

The longer we've gone without dealing with a trauma or pain, the more trauma or pain we accumulate. If this is the case, then there may be multiple things that hold you down. They will need to be addressed one at a time.

What is that one thing that you think about too much that causes you pain? Is it hurt from the past or a fear of something in the future? The problem with holding something from the past or the future is that it negatively affects your outcomes and mood in the present. The past is done, and the future doesn't exist yet.

It doesn't matter how often you think about a certain problem, the answers that you seek won't always be ready to reveal themselves to you when you want them to. The days that present us questions rarely align with the days that present our answers to those questions. But we try to force these answers and end up losing motivation and focus. Instead of living through the pain of something once, we live through it every day that we allow it to linger in our mind. We are hurting ourselves by continually entertaining something that hurts us. Sometimes we don't realize this, and sometimes we do it on purpose because we subconsciously believe we deserve some form of pain. We don't deserve any pain once we've found the lesson.

Going back to Rachel's story, she shared that many injustices had happened to her. She had suffered traumas and would relive them. Rachel often spoke about her "hit list," and who she would find and hurt one day. The people who had hurt her. The problem was that she was so focused on her past pain, that it severely clouded her judgement for the present and her direction for the future. She would relive the pain of her childhood trauma over and over long after the abuse had ended. The mind and the body remember trauma. It has a few techniques to deal with it. One way is that it can suppress trauma by pretending it never happened and hiding it in the recesses of our brain.

The problem with this method is that suppressed trauma can and will often leak out into other areas of our life. We may not know why we do certain things, but we continue to do them, this could be leaking trauma. Another way the mind deals with trauma is that it seeks closure or revenge. Before we talk about closure, let's look at revenge or hate (a negative form of closure). Rachel had a hit list because it gave her back some of the power that had been taken from her by the people that had hurt her. It was her way of ensuring an eye for an eye and thus getting the closure she wanted. One day we were driving to an appointment, and she was in a very negative headspace. She kept saying how she was going to hurt everyone that had hurt her.

I knew that she had gone over this way of thinking a thousand times before in her mind. It was eroding her future. She was planting weeds in her mind where she should have planted crops. I looked at Rachel and asked her to look in the rear vision mirror. She did. I asked her, "what did she see?" She said all the traffic behind her. I then asked her what would happen if she tried driving the car forward while only looking in the rear vision mirror; she said she would crash. I told her something I had heard years ago. I said to her that there is a reason the windscreen is much larger than the rear-view mirror — because we are only meant to take small glimpses at what is behind us to prevent it sneaking upon us, while our focus should be on what is around us and ahead of us. Rachel sat back into her chair quietly, deep in thought. She rarely spoke of her hit list after that except in a joking manner.

Finding closure is generally a healthy method of dealing with something. Revenge and holding pain are death by a thousand cuts because we relive it over and over. The problem with closure is that we want it now, but it doesn't always present itself in that moment, so often we live with pain and trauma until it does. What we learn is that we can apply our own form of closure when the closure we seek doesn't want to show up. We do this like all things through practicing to let go. We forgive the past and make a conscious decision to be our own best friend. To love ourselves enough to understand that we need to let certain things go. We tell our trauma that it no longer has control over our future.

The first time I missed out on qualifying for the Olympics I was devastated. I had trained so hard for so long and just missed out because my competitor beat me in the final match. I would have to wait another four years to have another shot. Only the Gold medalist from the Oceania region would qualify their country for the Olympics, I got silver. Not only that but I also spent three months in a wheelchair with a fractured bone and severely sprained ankle. That was my first real taste of defeat. It's hard to remain positive when you're in a wheelchair and just missed out on your lifelong dream to become an Olympian. It took me six months to really process and move through the pain.

I had chosen subconsciously to hold onto it and beat myself up over how close I got to qualifying but had just missed out. In that period, I learned many lessons including how to let go. It was done, and there was nothing I could do about it. Four years later I had another shot at the Olympics, and the exact same thing happened. I made it to the final and lost in the last round, again ending up on crutches and missing my Olympic dream. This time things were different; I had learned that holding onto the pain of defeat served me no good purpose. Unlike the previous time four years earlier, it took me just one night to feel the pain and then to move on from it. I had made the choice and learned the lesson of how important it was to let go. I partied that night with my coach and the competitor that beat me. I was happy for him.

This was a vital part of my growth as a person. And yes, it was as simple as making a choice. I had given my best, and it just wasn't my time, that's all I could do. The first time it happened, it took me six months of pain and the second time I missed out on my dream, just one night.

This lesson was one of my most valuable in life. That letting go of what was out of our control would bring so much more happiness. Four years later, I qualified and won that elusive Gold that made me an Olympian. I had learned that letting go and fighting through adversity was the cost that needed to be paid to achieve a dream.

Are you still holding on to that one thing? Or are there a couple of things? Do they bring you pain day after day? Find closure in letting go. If someone wronged you, then the laws of the universe, with its cause and effect, will deal with them. If you wronged yourself or someone else, then seek out good and kind ways to balance the karma that you've created. Do not dwell in negativity. If you continue to feel that pain, you are choosing to allow it to hurt you day after day. And if that one thing is a future fear, then the same applies. By focusing on a possible future pain, you also invite that future pain not only to happen but to hurt you every day. You can only fix what is in your control and what is in your control is how you deal with problems and what you chose to focus on. Do you focus on the pain or on the lesson?

There is not much more motivating than knowing that the one thing that would cripple you day in and day out no longer weighs you down. Cut the anchor and stop seeking the type of closure that will hurt you or is out of your control. Be okay creating your own closure by choosing to move forward with a smile.

There is very little in life more demotivating than depression and negative thinking. It is like the chicken and egg argument. Which came first the chicken or the egg? Depression leads to demotivation, and demotivation can result in longer depression and so on and so on. We need to break this cycle. And we have within us all the tools needed to do this. Out there, there is expert help which may advocate other tools to help you. Use the tools which work best for you. I have purposefully left out three major tools, exercise, meditation and healthy eating, as they are addressed later in the book, but they also will be at your disposal.

Be aware of the environment that you are in. Are the people around you motivating, or do they cause you pain? Have you been stuck living in the same demotivating home for years? Then seek to move. Often times, just a change in environment, with its symbolism of new beginnings, will help kickstart your positive and motivated life. Having something to focus on that is positive is therapy in itself.

Fighting your way through depression is a marathon and not a sprint. You will have ebbs and flows. But as you continue to fight, you will find that life starts to balance out and that the ebbs become less and less and, soon enough, all you will get are flows. It will be liberating knowing that you have many tools at your disposal to assist you on this journey.

Light that candle and let the fire within you light the way to the happiness that you deserve!

I found this one morning on one of the walls of our homeless shelter.

The Mind vs. The Body

"The body is a servant of the mind, but like a loyal servant it can be called upon to help the mind in times of difficulty."

Goal — The goal of this chapter is to look at how the mind and body should be aligned to work in unison to maximize motivational energy.

Are you not completing a task because your mind stops you, or is it your body that says no? Part of you wants to work on that assignment or project, but your body wants to stay on the couch or in bed. But then again, your mind controls your body. It's all so confusing. Let me simplify it. Motivation requires a mixture of spiritual, mental, and physical elements. For the sake of simplicity, we will focus on the mental and physical aspects here.

The body doesn't function without the mind, and the mind has nothing to move without the body. If nothing moves, nothing gets done. Every task you don't do is restricted by both the body and mind to various degrees. To live a motivated life, you must work on both your body and your mind. They are two parts to the same whole, and both need to be optimized.

To illustrate the relationship between body and mind let's break down the task of getting to an exercise session in the early hours of the morning. The night before, you decide that tomorrow's the day, the big day you will get back into training. You go to sleep motivated and wake up to find that you've slept in. You came up with excuses like it was too cold or hot or conditions weren't perfect. You're now late for work, and you've missed your training session. The cycle then continues. You do this again and again, and soon you've formed a habit of not going to training. Habits are hard to break. So was it your mind or your body that let you down? In this case, it was your mind. Or said another way. your self-discipline. or will power. let you down. Your body may have been tired, but your mind had the capability, but just couldn't get it over the line.

Most people think that exercise is training the body. The truth is that exercise first requires thriving spiritual and mental strength. Your new physique becomes a by-product of this spiritual and mental strength. Your spirit or soul craves for a better stronger version of yourself. The best version of you allows you to serve your higher purpose. For this to happen, it then calls on the mind to put in plans and processes to get you to exercise and eat correctly. Your mind, in the moment after your alarm rings in the early hours of the morning, makes a quick decision to either drag your body out of bed or to find an excuse as to why you should stay in bed. When you finally find yourself exercising the body, it's long after the mind has achieved its morning exercise. The takeaway being that mental strength and habits leads to physical strength.

When training to qualify for the Winter Olympics, I had many interesting moments. I remember one cold evening in the Austrian Alps. I had just finished eating a tasty pasta meal with my fellow cross-country skiing athletes representing Mexico and Chile. It was nine p.m., and the temperatures were a low, negative-twenty degrees outside, with thick and heavy snow falling fast. Visibility was very poor, but luckily for me, I was inside. Well, so I thought. I was sitting on the sofa with a full belly of food winding down after a hard days training. Whilst I was sitting there, I noticed a towering figure standing over me. I looked up to see Yona from Chile, the South American ski champion, standing in front of me all dressed up to ski. He had a headlamp on his head and was staring right at me. Straight away I knew what he was after, he wanted to go out into the cold darkness of an Austrian winter and have another training session. The last thing I wanted was another training session.

For a split second, I thought about how warm my bed was, and how hard I had already trained that day not knowing that Yona wanted a three-session day. I had a hundred reasons why I shouldn't train. It was dark and late; it was cold; we had just finished eating, and we had already trained twice that day; snow had covered all the ski tracks; I didn't have a headlamp, and the list went on and on. At that moment, my body had given up, and so I knew that it was up to my mind to either take my body to bed or out to training. All I had to do was take that first little step mentally, and the body would follow. To Yonas' delight, I stood straight up and, without saying a word, I got changed into my ski outfit. I found some masking tape and taped my phone to my belt and turned on its flashlight. A few moments later, we were out skiing in the dead of night. Funnily enough, Yona and Madroza disappeared deep into the woods within the first few minutes of us starting. I didn't see them until the end of the session — close to midnight.

It didn't take long for my body to feel renewed and for energy levels to grow and get me through the session. I had refused to allow a perceived tiredness in the body to control my outcome. I wasn't injured, and although there were many reasons why I shouldn't train, I only needed one why I should. I wanted to become a Winter

Olympian. All we need to achieve a task is one good reason followed by one small dose of action. My spirit and mind were strong. What is your one good reason? What would make you do the extra work required to achieve that reason? Articulate that reason before you get in a position where you are tempted to give up and take the easy road. Plan for the times that will challenge you, long before they arrive.

The story I used is one example of the mental battles that would go through my head each and every day. Whilst I may be a two-sport Olympian it would be untrue to say that I don't experience those battles within myself every day. The difference is that I have trained my mind and will power to the point that those battles are but momentary speed bumps lasting a matter of seconds. By training the habit of taking a single small step forward when I didn't want to, I have achieved many great things. But more importantly, so can you. All you have to do is do something however small towards that task, and your willpower will improve. If you do this enough times, being able to resist temptations or complete tasks becomes easy. People believe that you need huge steps to get motivated. It's not true, you only need small actions done consistently. This is how you keep drive and enthusiasm going long term.

Both the body and mind need to be at optimum levels to achieve a challenging goal. But here's a secret so listen carefully. If the mind isn't focused, then the body must step up and pay the price to accomplish the task. But if the body is unwilling, it is the mind that must pay the price. By pay the price, I mean that it must do the majority of the work to get the task started.

If one isn't working, then the other must take up the slack and do extra work until the price is paid. How do we do that? I'm glad you asked! When my body was tired in Austria, I needed to rely on the willpower of my mind. Anyone can train that will power by repeatedly saying yes when a task needs doing. The secret is that your mind doesn't have to focus on the whole task, nor do you have to accomplish the entire task. You focus on only a small portion of the task until your will power is built up to a point where it can handle bigger tasks. By focusing only on that first part, we train our willpower muscle, which moves our tired body. Forget the idea of completing the whole task straight away, this can be overwhelming. We complete the big task later on once willpower and habit have been developed and strengthened.

So what happens when the mind is tired and unfocused, but a task needs doing? In this case, the body must do the extra work to start the task off. For this to happen, we must split our mind into two parts. The part that does want to do a task and the part that wants to stay in bed. These two parts are in constant battle. Both of them can and will control our body. Which one is stronger at any given time will dictate whether the task gets done.

The reason the mind has separate parts goes all the way back to our evolution as a human species. As we evolved so did our brain. Instead of being happy with just food, sex and sleep we started asking questions about life and purpose and higher-level thinking. The simplistic monkey side of our brain didn't like this as all it wanted was instant gratification. It couldn't see the bigger picture. Once we started having higher levels of thought, we also opened ourselves up to a need for greater brain processing power to achieve the larger, more complex tasks. The lazy/lower thinking part of our brain got challenged by our new evolving higher thinking part of the brain. The lazy part that just wanted to do simple survival tasks now had a new threat who would constantly remind us that we should want more out of life.

The way to test these conflicting parts is simple; do nothing. If you sit on your sofa or work chair or in bed long enough, you will most probably start to have thoughts of what you should be doing. With these thoughts come feelings of guilt for the time you are wasting. The action part of our brain is attempting to override the lazy part. Our own brain is in conflict with itself. It's no wonder we sometimes feel unmotivated! Our body in times of tiredness sides with the lazy part of our brain and this balance tips us towards procrastination or not working on a task or goal.

The big question then becomes how do we tip the balance so that we are more inclined to have our body do what the motivated side of our brain wants? The answer is that we train it; train it by doing small motivated tasks first, and then building those tasks up in magnitude. Each time we feel we need to accomplish something we take a small step in that direction by telling our body to act. Our body, initially, knowing that the task is small — as we have broken it down — will serve our high thinking brain. We will then build momentum, and low and behold, the task gets done. With time, our ability to do the bigger tasks grows.

Our goal isn't to discredit our primal survival brain but to have the two parts work in unison and not in conflict. We acknowledge that there are times when our body should serve the survival-oriented part and times when it should serve our higher thinking part. If it had its way, it would want to do as little as possible, conserve energy, and mainly serve our lazy, survival brain. When I say lazy, I mean simplistic. The *lazy* side isn't always unmotivated when its main needs need fulfilling. People would travel halfway across the world to meet a potential lover yet struggle to spend time with their kids or work on their mental and physical health. When someone is hungry enough, they will leave the comforts of their home to find food. If they got really hungry, some may even silence the higher thinking/ethical part and steal food. The lazy, survival part of our brain doesn't consider all the other priorities that need completing.

* * *

Look Your Best

"Present yourself in a way that makes you feel strong. You are presenting yourself to impress yourself; the energy you put out when feeling strong will attract others to you."

To get motivated, we want to look and feel our best as much as possible. For some of us, looking and feeling our best requires motivation. It's a chicken and egg problem. Do we need motivation to look our best, or do we need to look our best to get motivated? So which comes first? The answer is that you should do the very best with where you currently are in life. If you want that job as a CEO of a large company, then you should wake up each morning and do your best to make yourself look and feel like a CEO. That can, but doesn't necessarily mean wearing a suit, it could mean dressing and self-grooming in a way that makes you feel internally powerful.

Some of the most influential and successful leaders of our time wear plain t-shirts and unbranded jeans. Your definition of how a CEO should dress is more important than societies' definition. So long as you can attract clients and present well at certain events, then it is entirely up to you how this should look. By certain events, I mean things such as a courtroom, business meeting etc. In this case, a suit may be your best bet.

Gone are the days of everyone looking a particular way in certain jobs. Whilst there may be company dress standards, your goal is to reach a point where you are the one that defines those standards. Aiming to be in a company without aiming to own or run the company is aiming too low. Remember it's your life and whatever makes you feel comfortable and strong whilst still being respectful to clients and company structure is how you should dress. When you are the CEO, then you can define the company dress code.

One of the first things I do in the morning is I dress for my day. As an athlete, this typically means training shorts and a singlet. I shower and get ready as though I was going to train. Most of the time I am going to train but on days I don't I still prepare as though I was, why? Because dressing and feeling like the ultimate athlete make me feel strong. Feeling strong makes me feel motivated and feeling motivated helps me get things done.

In Taekwondo, we have a uniform. Contrary to what I said earlier, it would be wrong of me to arrive at a Taekwondo session dressed in a suit, even if I felt strong wearing that suit. A lot of things have tradition and working within that tradition is part of what makes us feel connected to a group. That said, these days there are training times, especially in summer where even Taekwondo athletes wear partial uniforms. Even during these times, I would still wear a full Taekwondo dobok or at the very least, Taekwondo pants and my black belt. Wearing those pants and that belt would put me in the Taekwondo training zone and remind me that I am a high-level black belt, this would make me feel strong and give me a better training session.

Dress not to impress others but to feel internally powerful. How that looks for you is an individual matter. Your presentation to the world is the first thing people notice when they meet you. The energy, positivity, and how you make people feel is how they remember you.

Self-care and self-grooming are just as important for men as they are for women. A good haircut or beard trim can make any man feel better. There are countless stories of charitable Samaritans who help the homeless by providing free haircuts/showers or clean clothing. That little boost of positive feeling can be enough to make someone feel good about life. When you feel good, you also invite the motivation cat back into your life.

When I was thirteen, tragedy hit. I lost my grandmother, a beautiful and kind lady, to old age. I remember travelling to the outer islands of Tonga on a long boat journey to attend the funeral. What I didn't know was that I had just contracted the start of Dengue fever, a dangerous mosquito-borne virus similar in ways to malaria. The fever was so bad that once I arrived at the outer island, I couldn't even attend the funeral. I was that sick, and we had no access to medicine that my family was very concerned about what could happen to me. It was impossible to keep food down. The fever had me half delusional.

After a few days of being bedridden, I distinctly remembered two cravings I had. One was for a cold coconut and the second was for a shower. Instinctively, even in my sick state, I knew that a shower and a coconut would make me feel better. I remember whispering to my father if he could help me shower. He carried my frail body and sat me on the concrete shower bench and filled a bucket with water from the rainwater tank for me to use. The smell of the soap and the clean feeling did something extremely positive to my mood, it helped remind me I was in the land of the living. Father gave me a coconut to drink, and I started feeling better. Still, to this day, I use a shower as a form of a mental refresh. I felt clean and awake, and with a fresh change of clothes, I started to heal. Three days later I was on a boat back to the main island feeling much better. How do you feel after you have a shower and put on a fresh set of clothes? Motivation requires as many positive things to be in our favor. Let looking and feeling healthy and alive be one of those things.

* * *

Hormones

"Our hormones play a pivotal part in our motivation and emotions. Understand how they work, and you will better understand how you work."

The body is extremely complex. A lot of what we do is dictated by an intricate dance of chemicals within us.

Everything about us in some way leads back to the atoms and molecules that make up our being. Motivation isn't just a matter of thinking but also a matter of understanding what is happening physically when we think or feel a certain way. To be motivated we need to have at least a basic understanding of the chemistry that makes us tick. Meet the hormone.

A hormone is a chemical messenger within the body. It's like the postman delivering a message from one part of the body to another. Now there is another kind of postman known as the nervous system that also delivers messages. The nervous system postman is much faster than the hormone system postman because he uses the fast-flowing electrical roads of the nervous system. The hormone postman travels the slow and congested blood flow system to get to his target.

We know that a hormone carries a message but from where and why? I'm glad you asked! The short answer is that they carry messages that tell us to do something or to feel a certain way. For example, there are hormones that make us hungry, hormones that make us feel happy, and hormones that make us sleep or wake up, to mention a few.

Hormones are complex, and they affect different people in different ways. If you are not sure why you feel a certain way, or why your energy feels low, then have your hormone levels tested. Further your study on specific hormones and how they work for you. Stress, hunger, and sleep are all influenced by the intricate dance of these chemical messengers as you will see in the following sections.

* * *

Sleep

"The quality of our rest will dictate the quality of the goals we can achieve while we are awake."

Sufficient rest is one of the most undervalued parts of living a motivated life. Rest which includes sleep and meditation is when our body and mind has the opportunity to heal itself and process thoughts and feelings. Close to one-third of our life is spent in sleep. If one-third of our life is spent resting, shouldn't we then invest as much effort into optimizing that rest period as we put into the times that we are awake? Of course, we should! If we aren't getting sufficient rest, we aren't healing; if we aren't healing, then it's only a matter of time until our mind and body pay the price. There have been countless studies on the importance of good sleep for our health. People who get insufficient sleep appear to age quicker, get sick easier, perform daily tasks with less dexterity, and experience more stress, amongst other difficulties. If people don't get enough rest, then the times that they are awake, they are only functioning at a small percentage of their capability. It's hard to be motivated when the body needs rest.

To be a master of motivation, you must also be a student of sleep. The exact amount of sleep a person needs can range somewhere between six to nine hours per day. There are of course outliers whereby certain people need more or less sleep. A lot of science and whole books have been put into understanding sleep and sleep cycles. Be a student of knowledge and read as many of them as possible and trial methods that work for you. Creating a plan to get sufficient sleep is as essential as creating daily goals. Without sleep, you will struggle with any of your goals.

A commonly stated number is that we need eight hours of sleep per day. Whilst this is a good beginning number, it doesn't take into account different people with different daily tasks and energy expenditure. It also doesn't consider the realities of the modern world with high functioning individuals flying and moving in different time zones. Sometimes it just isn't practical to get the eight hours that we need, but we should try.

The purpose of this book isn't to get deep into the science but to simplify complex concepts into useable ideas. The best way I have found to find your required sleep number is to go to sleep relatively early after a busy day of physical and mental activity. Don't set an alarm and see when you first naturally wake up — assuming this isn't just to go to the restroom — then write down this number. Do this a few nights over a week to get a good average. Simple isn't it? Now, this doesn't always work for people who suffer insomnia, broken sleep patterns or have had a period of insufficient sleep leading into this trial.

What we want is a range that is healthy for us. One whereby we wake up naturally and feeling refreshed.

An alarm clock though sometimes necessary doesn't allow us to wake up at the right time of our sleep cycle. Our sleep cycle is basically our body clock that sets itself to the different cycles of sunrise, sunset, and, some believe, the moon's monthly cycle. It is a clock for turning on and off different processes in our bodies such as metabolism and healing. An alarm shouldn't be what wakes you up but the last line of defense against being late to work or an appointment. If you aren't waking up before your alarm, then you aren't going to sleep early enough.

Shift work can really take a toll on your body and mind. It may pay the bills for now but starting shifts in the middle of the night affects our body clock and thus impacts healing processes negatively. Why? Because humans have evolved to follow the rising and setting of the sun. Working shift work in the middle of the night throws this process off and, in the long run, will affect you negatively.

We know life isn't perfect and sometimes we will go through those moments and make sacrifices whereby sleep is hard to get. So long as what you are doing at the time makes progress toward getting where you need to be, by all means, continue. Just remember that the longer you go with insufficient rest, the greater the price will be health-wise.

In qualifying for the Olympic games, there were days when sleep was tough to get. I would need to wake up at five a.m. most days for training but wouldn't sleep until around midnight. This gave me only five hours of sleep per day for many months. What I found was that my actual performance, while I was awake, took a drastic dive. It would take me longer to heal from injury, and I didn't have the same level of energy and enthusiasm with each day. My increased workload mixed with my decreased sleep was a recipe for disaster. I was starting to burn out and starting to hate what I was doing. This was an early and scary warning sign that something was very wrong. Being self-reflective I was able to notice this trend and decrease in performance and associate it with my lack of sleep. I then took a few days completely free from training and just slept. What a difference it made.

After my slumber, I returned back with increased motivation, energy and drive. I spoke with my coach, and we factored sleep and recovery into the training plan. There were now sessions of time where I was only allowed to rest. This made all the difference. Are you feeling run down from all the stress and lack of sleep? If the answer is yes, then the cure is simple. Factor rest into your day and find ways to make sure it happens.

We can't talk about rest without also talking about meditation. Meditation is where you spend time looking inward and disconnecting from the world and its distractions. It is a form of rest and recovery. For some people, meditation can simply be a long slow walk with calming music or an audiobook. For others, it can be a quiet room with nothing but you and your thoughts. People of religion can use meditation as a form of prayer whereby they reconnect with the universe or their creator. Each person gets different benefits out of meditation, and each person meditates slightly differently even though there are commonalities.

I am a fourth-degree black belt in Hapkido a deadly form of Korean martial arts. One of the things we learned was that before and after every single training session we would meditate. This involved us sitting cross-legged on the floor with our eyes slightly open and our hands on our waist near our navel. In Eastern culture, this is your center. When we are born, all nutrients come from our Mother through this center, and so it has significant meaning in meditative practice. We did this for three to five minutes each time. In that time, I would do two things. Firstly, I would pray that my Hapkido session would be focused and effective. Secondly, I would park the issues of the day and of the World so that when it came time to start our session, I was completely present. Sitting quietly for a few minutes a day can make a drastic difference in your life. The goal we were taught with meditation wasn't to sort out our problems but to give ourselves time to be free of all problems, expectations, and troubles.

The best way I have found to think of meditation is this. Imagine if we hold a lightweight out in front of our body with our arms straight, it is easy. If we keep holding that weight, soon it feels heavier. If we hold it long enough, it starts to burden our life and cause us pain and struggle. Meditation isn't to help us hold the weight; it is to allow us to rest by placing it down. By putting down our problems each day, we then renew our energy to tackle them.

With meditation, find what works for you. Some people may end up falling asleep if they meditate for too long. While the goal isn't to fall asleep, if this happens then just go with it. Your body obviously welcomes the rest. There is no need to take something that's made to help you so seriously that you feel guilty for falling asleep. What I will say is that if this happens continuously, then just decrease the length of your meditation and avoid positions like laying down that facilitate sleep.

The most important physical need in life is oxygen, this comes before water and food. Stop breathing for a few minutes, and we die. This being the case it makes sense that learning how to breathe is vital. Oxygen nourishes all cells in the body and allows you to extract energy from the nutrients you eat. With decreased oxygen, our cells and our quality of life suffer. Like rest, we need to learn how to breathe properly. As we go through life, our body finds little shortcuts to use less energy. One of those shortcuts is shallow breathing. What happens over time is we stop breathing deeply and start breathing more shallow which decreases oxygen intake. Decreased oxygen leads to increased illness and lack of energy and motivation. During meditation, breathe deeply. The goal is to have your lower stomach expand out and thus draw air to the full area of your lungs. This is opposed to chest breathing, whereby shallow, up and down movements of the chest cavity result in less oxygen uptake. We may find that we revert back to our shallow breathing during the day but be aware of this and when it happens, take five deep breaths to remind our nervous system to breathe deeply.

While meditating, deep controlled breathing is vital. It increases oxygen, calms our nerves, and forces us to slow down from the pace of life. During our martial arts training, we would breathe deeply and slowly, and when it got time to spar or fight, we would find that we were also able to control our breathing to the point where we got maximal oxygen for minimal energy expenditure. It helped calm us in competition while maintaining a strong and effective fight pace. This I then went on and used in Cross country skiing. This form of skiing is the highest Vo2 max sports known to man. The amount of Oxygen uptake needed to engage in cross country skiing competitively is extremely high and very difficult for most people, myself included. Even though I wasn't a distance athlete, I had learned that calm, deep, controlled breathing could increase my performance and decreased my fatigue during a race. I wasn't controlled by the adrenaline of the moment but by the calmness I had learned from breathing deeply during mediation many years earlier at Hapkido and Taekwondo training.

Don't be fooled by poor information telling you that to be successful in life you need to sleep less and do more. This just isn't entirely true. An elite athlete can sleep for eight hours, train for four to six hours and still have ten hours to do life. Your awake time is already sufficient to make you successful so long as the quality of your awake time is high because you slept well. Unless you are over-sleeping, accept that your body needs rest to recover, especially if your day is filled with activity. To be successful in life, you need sufficient rest so that in the time that you are awake you are living at your best, tackling each daily task with vigor and motivation. Make sleep a part of your program, and your motivation levels will rise as you power through your day.

* * *

Age

"It's up to the Universe to decide how many years we have but up to us to decide what we do with those years. The best years are yet to come."

When I was nineteen, my close friend said to me, 'Get ready for your twenties, they will be the best years of your life.' They were. When I turned twenty-nine, he said, 'Get ready, because your thirties will be the best years of your life,' and they are. I have a very wise friend, and I know that whatever age I enter, he will say the same thing, and I will believe it.

When we are young, we want to be older, and when we are older, we want to be younger. So many people use age as an excuse to prevent their achieving goals and starting new things. They overvalue the biological clock and use it as a measurement of how they should approach life. They want to travel in their twenties, get married around their thirties, have a white picket fence and a few kids by their forties, and retire in their sixties. Life is planned out to a tee. The problem is that life also has its own plans. It challenges everything we do to see if we are worthy of the next step. Now there are elements of your biological clock that are very real. We do age. But we have more control over how we age than what we give credit for.

Some people get so caught up on age and length of life that they forget to focus on their quality of life. They think it is about the number of years and forget about the quality of those years. The ultimate being a combination of both.

I have seen ninety-year-olds run marathons and hundred-year-olds jump out of planes. I had an eighty-year-old uncle who would go spear fishing all alone in the middle of the night, in the Pacific Ocean, and return with a shark to feed the family. People are miraculous but short-change their own potential by saying things like "I am too old." The problem comes when they start to believe what they say, and it spills over into other areas of their life. They start with, "I am too old to play sports," and soon it leads to "I am too old to do…,"— insert task. Remember that your body is a servant of your mind. As you speak, so shall you be. Don't speak of everything you can't do but of all the good things you can and will do. Be a guardian of the language that you use with yourself and others.

If you want a motivation killing word, it's called retirement. Or more accurately, it's the commonly held understanding of what retirement is. What is it exactly that we are retiring from? If we made a decision to live our best life, then we should never want to retire, or withdraw, from the things that give our life flavor. Even language such as *the twilight years of my life* is unmotivating. One day we will pass on to the next life; let that happen naturally, and by all means, don't do or say things to encourage it.

Some people have lived a very tough life and spent most of it in grueling work. For these people, they deserve the opportunity to rest and enjoy the fruit of their labor. When this happens, we need to prepare for a sudden change in routine. If you spent your whole life working and then suddenly stopped, you may find that you lose purpose and motivation. Be ready for what you will do before each season of life comes. You don't store the wheat in winter but in summer, and in doing such, you create your action and activity plan long before you reach a point of no activity.

If you come to an age whereby you feel lost and uncertain, then this can be challenging. It may be menopause for women or some form of midlife crisis for men or women. You may hit a point where your life purpose or direction is challenged. Assume this will happen long before it does and plan for it. It's easier to go through a crisis when you have tools in the ready to negate the effects of the crisis or challenge.

There is a universal principal that affects anyone of any age; *use it or lose it*. This applies whether it be a physical movement or improving your memory and mental acuity. It is amazing how our body and mind adapts to the movement patterns and thoughts we put it through.

I spoke to a friend who had married in his early twenties. By his early thirties, he looked as though he had hit his fifties. He said that everything changes once you have children and once you "get older." I pressed him for more information as I found this way of thinking interesting and very common. He said that he had less energy and had put on extra kilograms and felt constantly unfit due to his age. He was only thirty-two at the time. I understood the biology of the human body and that certain processes such as testosterone production can decrease with age, but he wasn't even close to being in a bracket where this would become a measurable issue. And if he was in that bracket, then it could be addressed through healthy and natural testosterone boosting activities such as prioritizing sleep, specific nutrition and full-body, compound exercises; all shown to increase testosterone production. I had a lot of empathy for my friend and understood that in his mind he was finding reasons to justify *letting himself go*.

Humans are masters at justification. We strive to find ways to align our current life circumstances and choices with the story we tell us about ourselves in our minds. This is called reducing cognitive dissonance, i.e. if it's hard to change our habits, we then change our mental blueprint, and what we tell ourselves to validate our bad habits. It makes us feel better about our choices and is easier than to take the action needed to make real and positive changes.

I looked my friend in the eye and told him that the reason he wasn't moving and feeling as energetic as when he was twenty was because he wasn't exercising, sleeping or being as active as when he was that age. His children needed a healthy and happy father, and so he would need to increase the priority of his own self-care. He needed a complete overhaul of his belief pattern around ageing. If left to his own devices, he would have found himself further stuck in a loop and negative health spiral. He needed to continue to commit himself to learning to keep his mind sharp and use exercise and nutrition to keep his body healthy. He took the advice to heart and miraculously returned to a much healthier state within a year. Anything we don't use, we lose.

Movement patterns are another interesting aspect to aging. The body adapts to the specific movement patterns we put it through. That could be walking, sitting, or exercising. When I was living in Korea and training for the Olympic Qualifiers, I saw an elderly lady, most probably in her eighties, bent at the waist at an almost ninety-degree angle. She was walking with a shoulder harness attached to her upper body while dragging a cart of recycled plastic bottles. I noticed two things. One was that she maintained an activity-filled life which added to her longevity, and two was that years of bending at the waist and dragging that cart had resulted in her body adapting to that position. She couldn't stand upright. It looked as though she had worked so long that her upper torso stayed at almost ninety degrees. I would have loved to have seen her have a rest from a tough life of hard work and take on other forms of exercise. Her life circumstances meant that this wasn't to be at that stage. I was in awe of her energy as she pulled her cart through the narrow roads of Seoul.

The body finds ways to minimize energy, and it adapts to the movement patterns we put on it as we age. A common example is us bending at the waste and losing posture as we get older. If someone told me that this happens to everyone because of age, I would say that that's not a valid or specific enough reason. The real reason is multi-faceted and includes years of poor posture, movement patterns, a heavy head mixed with loss of muscle strength through the back and glutes, and an underactive core amongst other things. Adding in cumulative and untreated lifelong injuries with ailments like arthritis, osteoporosis or decreased bone density and joint problems further paints the picture that we call aging.

If we go through life and call our ailments the results of age, then we limit our ability to address the specific ailments that bring on our poor mental and physical condition. While we will all get older, we need to understand, proactively, exactly what is happening to our bodies and do our very best to correct what we can control in order to live a healthier life.

Look after the muscles and the joints that will take your body into its later years. Ensure full range of healthy movement through each joint long before you develop joint problems. Train your muscles to hold your posture and movement patterns, and they will continue to serve you through life. Read and constantly strive to learn more, train your mind the way you train your body, with stimulus and repetition. Use it or lose it.

That kid chasing the butterfly with a curious heart is where and who we should be throughout life. Constantly evolve and learn, and you will continually be rewarded with happiness and enriching lessons. Aim always to give back to those who are struggling, and you will find purpose and meaning.

Alcohol, Drugs, and Porn

"Everything that you consume will have an impact on your life. Only you will be able to understand, moderate, and control that impact."

Very few of us want to talk about our addictions. They often highlight the parts of ourselves that we would rather keep hidden from the world. They bring to our attention the inner battle we all face between the wolf of negativity and the wolf of purpose. The things that we are addicted to can bring us temporary highs, and thus make us momentarily feel good. The battle with addiction is one where we may at times be unsure as to what side we are on. With one hand, an addiction can give immediate joy, and with the other, it can rob us of long-term happiness. This chapter isn't about judgement or self-blame. It is purely about becoming self-aware in order to live a motivated life. We will then look at ways to address addictions.

Let's begin with a discussion on drugs and alcohol. It's a sensitive topic to talk about for someone who has never drunk or consumed recreational drugs. How could I ever understand the trials and tribulations of depending on something I had never consumed? How could I ever provide advice, if I had never experienced the highs and the lows. It was possible that I could run the risk of disconnecting myself from you by talking about such a topic. And what level of specificity would my statements need to have in defining what constitutes a *drug*? Would I go by the definitions given to us by society and country-specific laws? Or would I draw the line at a drug being natural vs. synthetic?

I have spent almost two decades observing, learning, working with, and creating effective solutions for thousands of recovering addicts from all walks of life — whether they were addicted to drugs, alcohol, porn, gambling, or even exercise that can, funnily enough, unbalance one's center. My life has provided me the opportunity to be well versed in this domain, and from this, I have crafted the RPM-TEN plan.

I have witnessed a lot of pain and suffering, and I would prefer not to see more. I have seen certain drugs take absolutely everything from someone and leave them with nothing. I have talked a number of people away from the edge of self-destruction all of whom were under the influence of drugs or alcohol.

Now, there are levels to substance use, levels to different substance strengths, and addiction potential. As you read this section, think about what your relationship is to substance use, and the raw reason as to why you consume such substances.

Your motivations for your current decisions around drugs and alcohol will be based on your personal experiences.

There are three alcohol-related experiences that really stand out to me as I look back on my life and the decision around not using it. They are vivid memories, and I share them to show you my processes on understanding how we as humans make current decisions based on past experiences.

When I was fourteen, we moved into our house on the main island of Tongatapu, not long after a cyclone wiped out our small one-bedroom home. It was late in the evening in the middle of summer. I heard a commotion outside as I was getting ready for bed. A large gathering of villagers had come down to the lagoon's edge with torches; some were crying, some with very nervous looks on their faces. Our house was right on the lagoon edge, and so I went down with my father and cousin to see what had happened.

Two men from the village had been drinking heavily throughout the day and decided to go for an evening swim. They hadn't returned. A number of villagers were wading through the lagoon with torches, yelling for the men to answer. Hours went by, when we suddenly saw some of the villagers wading back in the waist deep water. I walked out to meet them; they were silent. Behind them were the bodies of the two men who had been drinking and now had drowned.

The villagers were shaking, and I could hear the women on the shore wailing and crying. I reached down and helped drag one of the men onto land. He had turned blue, and his open eyes stared right up at me. I still remember that image and the cries of the villagers. It was a strange feeling seeing something like that. The two men drowned in waist high water after consuming excessive alcohol.

The second traumatic experience was when I was in boarding school. I had a great Brazilian friend who was the life of the party. Wherever he went, people would laugh at his love of life and hilarious joke filled mannerisms. He was good natured and always appeared happy. One afternoon, he left the boarding school to go to a party with his sister. That was the last I saw of him. He had had a lot to drink and returned to the dormitory in the early hours of the morning. After returning heavily intoxicated, he was given a stern talking to by one of the boarding masters. I walked out of the dormitory at seven in the morning and saw my older brother, who was also a boarding master, stopping all the students from going to breakfast. He looked at me and didn't say a thing.

I knew something was wrong. A few hours later, the head of the boarding school informed us that my good friend had passed away after falling from the four-story-high chapel after a night of drinking. We were shocked and couldn't believe that one day he was here, and one day he wasn't. I believe that he was suffering from some form of internal conflict that we didn't know about; alcohol had magnified the pain that he was going through. I started to dislike alcohol even more.

My third experience came in my second year of university. A few of my friends and I were out celebrating a night on the town with my brother. We had just left a bar in the city of Brisbane on our way home when a large group of twelve drunken men attacked my friend for "looking at them funny." We had no idea what had happened, but within seconds, there was a group of men standing around him after he had been knocked to the ground. They were attempting to kick him while he was down. I turned to see my brother and our friend from Papua New Guinea jumping into the madness while another friend bolted for safety. I had avoided fighting and violence like the plague. At this stage in my life, I was extremely calm from years of martial arts training and had nothing to prove. I had no need to show any inflated ego.

All of my fighting was done in the ring. But here was my unconscious friend suffering as the men senselessly attacked him. As a last resort, I leapt into action. I stood with one foot on each side of his head to shield him while fighting off the attackers in the middle of the road. At that point, the leader of the group reached inside his black leather jacket and pulled out a gun saying he was going to shoot me in the face. After remembering the line from an old western cowboy movie, I told him to make sure he got me good, because if he missed, it would be the last thing he did. At this stage, all of his friends had run away after my brother and our Papuan friend had unleashed some form of Polynesian attack that had the men running. The leader of the group, after seeing his comrades scatter, also turned and ran. I remember picking up my friend and watching his dazed, blood covered face as he came to. What was meant to be a great night out could have gone horribly wrong and all because of a group of men who'd had too much alcohol.

Again, your motivations for your current decisions around drugs and alcohol will be based on your personal experiences. This isn't to say that one decision is wrong, and one is right. It is to say that you should try to understand your motivation behind everything you do, including your level of alcohol or drug consumption. Can you drink to a point where you can enjoy your evening, or do you find you drink in excess and struggle to remember the night? Are you drinking to enjoy the company of others or to drown your sorrows and avoid some pain? Only you know your drinking limits; only you know if you continually go over them. Look back on your life, and what your relationship is with alcohol.

What mental program are you running around drug and alcohol use? Is it for personal entertainment and joy or is that joy to mask some past or current pain? Did your parents consciously or subconsciously impart drinking behavior and culture upon you? Or was it your peers? Is it benefiting your life or taking from it? There is true freedom in being able to reach a natural high just because you love your life. Substance use can only mask pain and trauma for so long. Imagine a life where you were in complete control over both your happiness and your health, that is the life that you deserve.

* * *

Porn

This is a very sensitive topic among the male population, and one that is rarely written about, yet is extremely prevalent in modern society. Porn addiction is something that will, in time, prove to be a big problem to the motivation of an individual and health of relationships.

I grew up before the internet was a thing. My expanding adolescent brain was absorbing nature and fishing and school and farmyard tasks. If any of the guys at school had pornography, it was in the form of still images from an adult magazine that they had stolen from an unsuspecting uncle. But times have changed, and technology has brought with it a multitude of problems including porn addiction. Now, this isn't an ethical or moral chapter. It's purely about the negative motivational effect that porn consumption can have on some men and potentially their partners. I say men because it is largely a male problem. Overuse can cause dissatisfaction within a relationship and decreased virility. This can then lead to feelings of unworthiness or blame whether it be toward a partner or oneself.

The majority of men are quick visual processors of erotic imagery, and pornography exploits this visual inclination. Some of the companies that produce it even have psychologists and producers teaching actors how to move, and what to say, to maximize the viewer's stimulation response. If we want to find a motivation killer, it could very well be excessive porn use.

Typically, women tend to view porn much less often than men do. They are more inclined toward storylines in romance novels, or erotic description, sometimes for entertainment and sometimes for escapism or excitement. Addiction to anything whether porn, alcohol, drugs etc. is largely an addiction to the happy feeling of dopamine release.

So how and why does this work? The simple version is that we have a special feel-good hormone called dopamine. We get a release of dopamine when we are rewarded for something. When we have pleasure-filled situations like orgasm, dopamine is released. What happens with porn is that men are exposed to thousands of different dopamine-releasing erotic images from the comfort of their computer or phone and in a very short time. They can click from one person to the next and thus have an endless variety of partners. Our brain hasn't evolved to meet this over-stimulation of dopamine nor can it necessarily differentiate between the person on the screen and one in real life. This can result in some men becoming addicted, and their brain decreasing their dopamine receptors. Fewer dopamine receptors mean a heavy porn user now has to find a more varied and extreme subject matter to get the same level of dopamine high. And so they spiral further into the addiction on their quest for this high.

Most addictions follow a similar dopamine high and then dopamine receptor regulation. Drugs such as cocaine or alcohol have the same effect. People build up a tolerance to the drug and thus need more to get the same hit. Our once motivated person now spends their time hidden away with their computer seeking more and more novelty. They stay up late and miss sleep, and their focus moves away from long term goals into immediate gratification. Without even realizing it, they are training the habit of seeking immediate gratification over long term happiness. This can spill over into other areas of their life.

Motivation and relationships can suffer from such an addiction. In the homeless shelters, there was no topic of education we would avoid. When people have problems or questions, it was up to us to address them in a way that made them feel comfortable but also to educate them. I saw porn addiction happening in young adolescent minds, and I worried for the future of these young people regarding having and maintaining healthy relationships. If a male was seeking an ever-increasing variety of pornographic stimulation, then what chance did a singular person have of fulfilling the needs of their porn addicted partner?

It is an evolutionary trait for humans to want to reproduce, and why this addiction can be very strong. It leverages a person's primal need in a way that may eventually hurt them. The solution, just like any addiction, is first an understanding of the addiction. Does the consumption of excess amounts of pornography serve your medium and long-term goals? If you experience a feeling of lethargy and lack of drive, then look at all your habits. Are you able to moderate your use, or does it spiral out of control?

This is about being self-aware and brave enough to question whether it affects your life and motivation, positively or negatively, and then to act on it. Giving alcohol to an alcoholic is often a slippery slope, and likewise, the porn user may decide to slowly remove that temptation and start building up their resistance to its use.

Swap the habit with healthy habits and seek ways to have real fulfilling experiences and relationships with real people. Whatever your decision around porn use, see an individual for who they truly are as a person and not just as a tool for immediate gratification. Everyone is a human being deserving of love. Becoming your greatest version requires love and an appreciation of people for their character and not just their physical attributes.

* * *

Beat Addiction with RPM-TEN

In all my years working with addiction, I have found certain processes that work extremely well. Almost all addiction is similar in how it affects our dopamine reward circuitry. The more information we have for understanding our addiction, the easier it becomes to overcome.

Below, I highlight my RPM-TEN plan to help overcome addiction that I have developed over many years working with addicts and counseling some of the most difficult cases at the homeless shelters. I have also applied the plan many times to my own life, to make sure that any negative addictions are regulated before they can take hold, and to ensure I remain balanced in areas such as exercise, healthy eating, and so forth, which can also be addictive if not moderated. Feeling guilty when consuming an ice cream every now and then or for missing a day of exercise because of family commitments isn't healthy — as life is also meant to be enjoyed. Everything should be in moderation, and everything to serve your longer-term goals.

The RPM-TEN plan:

Recognize the addiction

Prioritize your growth

Make a Master plan

Trade out the habit

Excuse or forgive relapses

Never quit on yourself

1 — Recognize the addiction

Addiction affects motivation because it takes away valuable time, focus, and mental resources from us achieving our goals. When most people think of addiction, they immediately think of drugs and alcohol, or food. There are many other things that we may be addicted to and not even know it. This step is about shining a light on areas where our mental blueprint follows an addiction pathway. This pathway pulls us to continually do certain things whether good or bad.

The first step in overcoming addiction is to recognize whether we are, in fact, addicted to one or many things. The goal is to audit everything that may have a negative impact on our life. What we want to do is recognize and list the things which we have been conditioned to over-use.

Some of these things include:

- Alcohol
- Recreational drugs
- Food
- Exercise
- Work
- Pain medication
- Relationships
- Drama or Gossip
- Shopping
- Gambling
- Plastic Surgery
- Social Media
- TV
- Telephone

Now this list isn't close to exhaustive. And notice how I didn't use descriptive words before the addiction. I could have said excessive exercise or toxic relationships or too much alcohol. This process isn't about passing judgement on the addiction but just recognizing the things that take up a lot of our time and energy. It may be difficult to bring your own addictions to light. This step will require you to be honest with yourself. Go ahead and list the things that you may be addicted to whether you feel them to be positive or negative.

2 — Prioritize Your growth

Once you've recognized the things that you are addicted to, the next step is to decide what it is that you want to do about these addictions. Your goal here is to prioritize your growth by determining what helps and what hinders you as a person. There are three things that you can decide to do with regards to your addictions, they are:

- Overcome and remove the addiction
- Moderate the addiction
- Ignore the addiction

1) Overcoming the addiction is where you make a conscious decision that it has a negative impact on your life, and that you would like to completely remove it from your life. It could be that it takes away energy or focus. It may cause pain to you or someone you love. If it is a drug addiction, then it may lead to highs followed by feelings of depression; it may have you becoming someone that you don't want to become.

2) Moderating the addiction is where you decide that there may be partial benefits to having the addiction if you can moderate how it affects you. Having an exercise or food addiction would fit in this space as removing exercise or food entirely would lead to negative outcomes.

Moderation is about balance. It is about acknowledging that some addictions may very well be beneficial if used for self-growth. Exercise can be a great addiction to have. But if you're at the gym six hours a day at the detriment of time with family, then you may decide to moderate it in order to keep your life balanced. This could also be the case with over training. Something I have done many times in my life. I look back on all the times that I over trained and the costs that I had to pay for doing this. My exercise addiction helped get me to the Olympics which is an amazing benefit; on the flip side, it also resulted in failed relationships. My partner would feel disconnected because I was often away, whether at the gym, competitions, or overseas training camps. On top of this, my exercise addiction resulted in many injuries that could have been prevented.

Prioritizing growth meant that I had to find ways to moderate my exercise and balance it with an active social, relationship, and family life. The interesting thing with moderation is that one of the answers to a failed relationship may be a mixture between moderating certain addictions and finding a partner who has a similar positive addiction. Addiction doesn't have to be bad. It just has to be understood.

A word of caution: moderating certain addictions can lead to relapses in people with an addictive personality. In all my time working with heavy drug and alcohol addiction, I rarely found a recovering addict who could drink or consume heavy drugs *sometimes* and not experience relapse or a downward spiral. There are reasons they became addicted in the first place and this was a mix of addictive personality and an addictive substance. Be careful about what addictions you want to moderate and what addictions you want to remove.

3) The third thing you can do is to completely ignore the addiction. This is not recommended, especially if the addiction leads to negative outcomes. Ignoring an addiction that harms you can make it much harder to deal with an addictive habit later on.

If overeating is your vice, and you do so when stressed, then you may believe that it is better to completely ignore your overeating during times of stress because, in your mind, it allows you to feel better in that moment. Remember that motivation requires us to prioritize medium to long term gain over immediate gratification. If we ignore the addiction, then it will be that much harder to address it at a later stage. The longer we ignore it, the more habitual and ingrained into our personal blueprint it becomes.

Prioritize your growth by deciding which addictions you want to overcome, moderate, or ignore.

3 — Make a Master Plan

Now that you've recognized your addictions and decided on how you would like to address them, the next step is to create a *Master Plan* that you can undertake to overcome or moderate the addiction. This master plan is a series of questions and steps that you create to assist you in controlling your positive habits and defeating your negative habits. The following questions and steps are on the assumption that you want to remove the addiction entirely.

Have you tried to quit before?

Perhaps you have tried quitting a negative addiction and it hasn't quite worked.

Have you tried a cold turkey approach or a slow cut?

For some people, going cold turkey is the best way to beat an addiction and for others it requires a longer-term approach. I had a close friend who was a heavy drinker his whole life until one morning he woke up completely naked, lying outside his house in the bushes after a night on the town. His shoes were lost, his pants were in the tree, and on his phone were pictures of random people he never remembered meeting. His child, after seeing him outside, walked out in the early hours of the morning and tried to wake him up. He had no recollection of how he got there and was so upset with the example he was setting for his kids that he quit all alcohol there and then. He never looked back and has been dry ever since.

A cold turkey approach often works for people who have extreme mental strength, or who have an experience that is extremely negative — as in the case of my friend who woke up in the bushes. The thing about mental strength is that there are times in our life where it may suddenly dip in power. This could happen around the loss of a loved one, financial problems, or some life crisis. It's easy to be strong when everything is going well. Being strong when everything is going wrong is the true test.

The slow cut is what I see as the more universally effective method. It mixes in elements of the cold turkey approach but with the acknowledgement that beating an addiction may need more than one attempt. Now this isn't to say that we should aim for multiple cold turkey approaches but that we should acknowledge that it may happen this way. The best outcome is a cold turkey approach followed by no relapses. The reality will probably see multiple cold turkey approaches followed by relapses and eventually success.

Is your addiction based on numbing, temporary pain?

Many addictions start when people seek something to make them 'feel good' during a time of pain. Alcohol, drugs, porn, and food are classic examples of this. There are other reasons people may trial something and later become addicted. It could be because of peers or some random set of circumstances that had them try an addictive substance or habit and then become hooked.

Alcohol, drugs, porn, and food are great at masking pain, but only temporarily and at a cost to self and relationships. If your addiction is a mask for pain, then part of your master plan will require you to deal with the source of that pain. It would still take work but would be much easier to give up an addiction, if the originating reason for that addiction is dealt with. There are many tools in this book to help you deal with pain. That said, professional counselling can be a great step to address and manage the pain's causes.

What are the thoughts and feelings you go through when you get a craving?

Journaling and writing down thoughts help frame them in a clean and clear light for you. There is therapy in journaling.

Understanding the sequence of thoughts and feelings that lead to you acting on your addiction is a powerful tool in your master plan. What triggers a craving? What justifications run through your head after the trigger? And what thoughts and feeling do you experience after indulging in the addiction? There is so much power in understanding why you do what you do. It allows you to throw a spanner in the works during any step between the craving trigger and the addictive task. All you need is one redirection or addiction swap at the right time to help you. List down everything that goes through your mind during your lead up to the habit. You may be surprised at just how repetitive those thoughts are each time it happens.

Who are the people that you surround yourself with?

I've addressed this in the removing negative influencers chapter. The people you surround yourself with can have a massive impact on your ability to overcome an addiction. It's easy for alcoholics to drink around other alcoholics. Drug addicts also gravitate to other drug addicts and so forth. We validate our decisions and decrease cognitive dissonance by being around people who are making similar decisions as us, whether right or wrong. Make an audit of the messaging your peer or family group is giving you.

Perhaps your peer group is a positive influence, but the habit is strong. Sometimes your addiction is completely personal and often an area of shame that you, for whatever reason, decide not to share with your peer group. This is normally because you don't want to be judged, or you're still in a contemplation stage as to whether you even want to overcome the addiction.

On a personal note, I've always found that two heads are better than one, and three are better than two.

Sharing your struggles with people who you have complete trust in is a sure way to get better information that could assist you in creating your master plan. I was never good at sharing my struggles. I thought that a man needed to do everything alone. It was liberating when one day in my early-twenties, I blurted out what I was struggling with in a relationship to a close friend and also to my brother. To my surprise, instead of being judgmental, they were extremely understanding and gave me some great advice. I then started to open up to a handful of trusted people about my challenges. What I found was that the information I was getting, along with the feeling of being able to verbalize problems, was liberating and therapeutic. It turns out that many people are also going through, or have gone through, similar problems. We aren't the first to have them, and we won't be the last.

4 — Trade Out the Habit

A vacuum by nature will seek to be filled. If not filled, then it will continue to pull elements or thoughts towards it. Our mind, once a thought or addiction is removed, becomes like a vacuum. This is one of the reasons that young kids absorb information around them so quickly. To just quit an addiction without having some other project or undertaking to take its place will make quitting even harder.

If the addiction is heavy drug or alcohol use, then what will take its place? What I have found as being the single greatest tool for overcoming an addiction is to help the person with the addiction find new and exciting projects or goals to focus on. One of the most effective tools for heartache, depression, or mental pain is to focus in on something that the person has a natural passion for. In Rachels story, she found photography, and so her focus moved to the excitement of that and away from drugs. The goal isn't to match the high of the addiction with the new undertaking, but to swap out the habit with something that re-absorbs a person's focus. This isn't about just redirecting focus in order to avoid thinking about a craving for the addiction. It's about working on our foundations to ensure that our purpose and life direction become the priority.

Prepare and undertake new and exciting ventures. Attend courses on anything even remotely interesting to you. Meet and link up with new people at these courses. List the hobbies or goals you've always wanted to accomplish. Healthy exercise and meditation are also great tools to help you realign your life and make you feel good in the process.

As you swap out the old habits for new healthy ones, you will find that your self-love starts to increase. You will feel the momentum of progress and will become addicted to self-development. What a great addiction to have!

5 — Excuse and Forgive Relapses

Being able to forgive yourself is a powerful tool. I speak more on it in a later chapter. With regard to addiction, it is extremely helpful for the addict's progress to be able to forgive themselves every single time they relapse.

We are, by nature, very good at being hard on ourselves. This can be powerful motivation or, if not used properly, can be detrimental to us overcoming our vices. Relapses can and do happen. Instead of self-punishing, give yourself a high five for the progress that you have made. For most of us, the goal of overcoming addiction is to undertake the addictive habit less and less frequently until it is a problem of the past.

What we want to do is avoid the "stuff it" response. The "stuff it" response is when you relapse so many times that you start to believe that you aren't able to overcome the addiction leading you to say, "Stuff it," and give up trying. This can then spiral someone into a dark place where they lose elements of self-worth.

Perhaps the first time you gave up alcohol, you lasted a week. The next time may have lasted a month. You then may have hit a rough patch and hadn't the tools to power through it, and so you fell back into heavy drinking. Whenever this happens, you have two options. You can self-hate, or you can congratulate yourself on the progress that you did make, and then try again. Forgive yourself each and every time and maintain the frame that you will overcome your addiction one step at a time. And that each time you try will be one step closer to your success at taking your life back.

6 — Never Quit on Yourself

You heard it right; the best way to quit is to never quit on yourself. I have never seen someone who had the right tools, and who made the clear choice to overcome an addiction, not overcome that addiction. Yes, I saw many relapses, but so long as they were striving to work on themselves, these relapses never stopped them.

Remove the temptations that trigger relapse. The motivation cat won't visit you, if you surround yourself with angry dogs. Audit the people around you to see if they help or hinder your quest. Decide on how you want your life to look.

This is the shortest but most important part of the RPM-TEN plan. Never quit on yourself. You are unique, and you are special. You deserve a life of clarity, freedom, and happiness — free from all negative addiction.

Lust, Sex, and Love

"One of our strongest primal motivators is the search for a partner. This search may give us our greatest pain but also our greatest joy."

There is very little more motivating than love, lust, and sex. I remember as a child reading a famous story about Helen of Troy. She was said to be the most beautiful woman in the world. Her beauty caused her lover, Paris, to steal her away from her husband, King Menelaus. The king, infuriated by this, sent a thousand ships of warriors to get her back — so began the story of Troy.

Whether it was love or lust that caused Paris and Helen to escape from Troy isn't important. What is, is that the feeling of connection they had was so strong that it was enough motivation to risk war and countless lives for them to be together. Now Menelaus was also driven by emotion. A mixture of jealousy, anger, and love had him motivated enough to send thousands of troops to their death to get Helen back. Emotions are powerful motivators, and love is one of the strongest emotions someone can ever feel.

Sex and love are motivating. There are no two ways about it. People do extreme things in search of their soul mate, and nearly as extreme things in search of someone to satisfy their sexual needs. I can almost guarantee that many of you reading this will be able to look back on your life and laugh, or cringe, at some of the things you have done in pursuit of love or sex.

Why is that drive to fulfil this need so strong that it makes otherwise calm people act irrationally? Let's first look at Love. I believe that there are two elements to romantic love. One is a spiritual connection to another human being. It is an unquantifiable feeling. Secondly, there is the physical chemistry that happens during a loving bond.

Firstly, we will look at the chemistry behind the connection with someone you love. In its initial stages, love starts as lust or attraction for someone. We make a conscious or subconscious decision that the person we have met has physical mating potential, and so we lust for the person. When this happens, we release hormones, the two main ones being testosterone and estrogen:

Testosterone — Testosterone is an androgen also known as the male sex hormone. Men produce it largely in the testes, while women produce it, to a much lesser extent, in the ovaries. Testosterone helps in the development of muscular strength along with increased libido.

Estrogen — Also known as the female hormone. In Women, estrogen is responsible for regulating the menstrual cycle and in men estrogen is needed in smaller amounts then testosterone to help facilitate fat loss, modulate libido and erectile function.

That attraction leads to a release of other hormones that include adrenaline, dopamine, and serotonin:

Adrenaline – Adrenaline increases the heart rate and thus supplies more blood flow to the body. Pain is decreased, and you feel like you are in a state of readiness. When this happens, you are physically and mentally at a heightened level of awareness.

Dopamine – Dopamine is the reward or feel good hormone.

Serotonin – Also known as the happy chemical. Most antidepressants regulate serotonin in some way.

Once we bond with the person we are in love with, we release another set of hormones mainly oxytocin and vasopressin:

Oxytocin – This is also known as the love and bonding hormone. It is a powerful feel-good hormone that helps two people socially connect and understand each other. What is really interesting is that it is released in large amounts during orgasm and also during childbirth. During orgasm, it allows for the couple to feel a loving and deep connection. During childbirth, it facilitates a powerful bond between the mother and child.

Vasopressin – From a love perspective, vasopressin and its receptors in the brain are also responsible for forming a connective bond between two people. There are theories that different levels of vasopressin can be what makes different people more motivated to stay in committed single partner relationships and others less inclined to.

Now, this hormonal release process can happen over a long time or in a short amount of time, as is the case when bonding occurs early. Each individual will be different. Looking back on my life, I would fall into the category where love and strong connection takes time. I believe this is because of my questioning/critical and extremely patient nature. But I also believe it could be because I wait to see if the test of time and hardship deters a potential partner. Understanding your method of connecting with a partner will give you more tools in your awareness of self, toolbox.

It's not important to remember all these hormones by name, but it is very important to know that the release of many powerful hormones happens during our search for love. The dance of these hormones influences our motivation.

Going back to looking at true love, I also mentioned that I believe that there is a spiritual aspect to the connection between two people. This is much harder to measure than a chemical connection, and so, from a logical perspective, challenges my engineering brain. But logic doesn't always explain complex issues like love. Have you ever been thinking of someone when suddenly, you receive a message from them? Have you ever met someone that feels so familiar as though you've met them before? Perhaps our love radar is so in tune to the emotions of particular individuals that we feel when they feel. The universe is complex, and we don't have all the answers, but we do experience unquantifiable feelings that surpass our current understanding of science.

Love is our greatest feeling, and loss of love is also one of our greatest pains. There is little in this world more painful than losing someone you love. It is something we will all experience at some stage. It is one of the constants of life. Don't fear it. My father always said that part of life is loss. Learn to deal with the loss in a healthy manner, and you will gain strength for a happy life. You will also learn to appreciate the times you do have with someone you love.

Pita Taufatofua

During my qualification run for the Winter Olympics, I lost three uncles and two aunties all in the space of a year. Within months of my uncle passing, my beautiful aunty Siu also passed. Siu was my father's sister, carved from the same cloth as him. She was full of love and energy. She went through life with a terrible lung condition resulting in her coughing constantly. She never complained about anything. She was the epitome of female strength and compassion all rolled into one. Once her husband Pita Pua passed, it wasn't long until she also passed. Heartbreak and that special connection stopped her fight; she was ready to join her husband in the next life.

I was sitting at the Winter Olympics when she passed; she saw me march out carrying the flag of Tonga, and a few days later she was gone. At her funeral, my uncle Uili, her brother, was so heartbroken and lost with grief that he also passed away. I flew back for his funeral to say goodbye but also to keep an eye on my father and to make sure that he was okay. Love and heartbreak are powerful things and, while we think we know how they work, there is so much we don't know.

Just because love can end in pain doesn't mean that we should avoid love. Dulling such a beautiful emotion to avoid possible pain of a later one can rob us of life's greatest gift. When you have love in your life, embrace and value it. Enjoy it while it is there and allow yourself to feel the highs it can bring. It may seem easier to give up the love we have for someone when we lose the person we love. This would make dealing with the pain of loss easier. That said, it's also still very okay to lose the person but not lose the love for that person. If there is a real spiritual connection, then this bond can't be lost.

The Motivation Station

Aunty Siu passed away while I was at the Winter Olympics in Korea.

Nutrition

"Food, first and foremost, should be about providing nourishment and fuel. Everything that you consume will at some point have an impact on your body."

Goal — The goal of this chapter is to understand the importance of nutrition in ensuring our body and mind functions at its optimum levels.

For good motivation and energy levels, our mind and our body must be at peak condition. What we consume information wise nourishes our brain and what we consume food wise nourishes our body. Try focusing on a goal or completing a task when you are hungry, it's not so easy. Try focusing or completing the same task after you over consume too much food and need to sleep, again it doesn't work. We need the right balance of nutrition that works for us.

As a professional athlete, I have had a lifelong study of nutrition. What we put into our body has the most important outcome on our overall health, physical and mental well-being. But why do I have to be an athlete to have this understanding? Why is it that everyone who consumes food, i.e. all of us, doesn't also have a deep understanding of nutrition? While my goals as an athlete may be different, eating is something we all do, but few understand. Your journey to understand food and its impact on your body will never end. There is no finish line as foods will change, scientific knowledge will update, food access will change, and your body and goals will also change. What you will get in this chapter is a better understanding as to how you can adapt your nutrition to meet your motivational goals. You will then go on your own personal journey to understand the nutrition habits that work for you. The study and understanding of nutrition will literally save and increase the quality of your life. You will be better positioned to achieve your goals as your energy and health improve.

I will be providing somewhat of a signpost as to where you should look to get nutrition information, but I will also give you some basic knowledge that you can apply immediately. The reason I can't give you specific information is that each person's body, goals, genetic makeup, illnesses, or conditions are different. Ultimately you are responsible for what you consume. Now let's get going and make this easier for you.

Nutrition is something that we can change immediately and will have a great impact on our life. Let's be completely honest with ourselves and strip away the gentle talk. It is easy to look at someone and immediately have somewhat of an understanding of their value system and level of discipline around nutrition. I would love to say that the world is fair, but it isn't. People are judgmental by nature, and first impressions count. We all owe it to ourselves to maintain optimal weight and thus health. If this has been a struggle, then your self-discipline muscle will require work. But you most certainly will be able to reach a point where nutrition and weight management are simple.

Now the goal is not to appease other people's visual judgement but to ensure that our health is at its optimal level of being. Obesity is an issue that is destroying people's lives. The reason I start here is that I come from a part of the world that has significant health problems associated with obesity. In the Pacific where I am from, we have high levels of cardiac disease, diabetes, and preventable illnesses. I have seen many family members pass away from diseases and conditions that could have been prevented or alleviated with proper nutrition. My care for you as a reader is in how you feel and how healthy mentally and physically you are. We need to optimize your nutrition levels to optimize your motivation levels.

As a UNICEF Goodwill Ambassador, I came across some shocking statistics around health. When informed, I couldn't believe that one in five people in the Pacific region experiences stunted development — both physical and mental. Not only are they shorter, but their brain development is impaired. Why is this the case? In the first two years of life from conception, the child has poor nutrition due to a lack of understanding or resources from the parents. It's a scary statistic that one in five kids in a whole section of the world will be stunted for life, not by their own choosing, but by lack of good nutrition in their first two years of life. The impact on motivation for these people is completely unfair because they didn't choose what they ate through their childhood, their parents did. We must understand nutrition not just for ourselves but for our families.

Different people have different goals. On a personal level, I have had to address nutrition to increase my weight but also to decrease my weight and to maximize health. When I took up cross country skiing, I was close to forty pounds heavier than the average skier. My Taekwondo physique was not going to help me with the goal of becoming a Winter Olympic athlete. I would need to lose weight. Every extra pound in a long-distance race adds up. And so, with my knowledge of nutrition, I went to work to shed a lot of body fat and unrequired muscle to reach my race weight. I removed over twenty-five pounds from a body that didn't look like it had twenty-five pounds to lose. This was my physical sacrifice, and I did it through exercise and nutrition.

I had to change years of eating habits and my diet to do this safely. Whereas before I could eat certain levels of carbohydrates, now that had to change. Losing hard earned muscle is an athlete's nightmare. We spend years trying to put it on. So when I had to remove that muscle, it was psychologically challenging. Everything in me wanted to maintain and grow the muscles not shrink them. My goals required sacrifice and so will yours.

Whether your goal is to lose weight, gain weight, increase energy, or to alleviate certain medical conditions, then you need to know what impact everything that you consume will have on your body. You will find that there are studies that contradict each other and further confuse you. Generally speaking, peer-reviewed scientific literature will give you good information. That said, some of these studies are funded by companies with vested interests in specific outcomes. What this means is that as you learn more, you must also have an understanding of the methods used to get that information. If, for example, you read a study that says certain fats are good for you, then you should also read the parameters of that study.

The group of people tested may not be in your age range, the sample size (number of people tested) may be small, or the test group wasn't people at all but lab mice. Now if you are like me and want good information and quickly, then there is no need to spend days reading scientific literature on food. Instead, find simplified meta-analysis write-ups.

Basically, what this means is that there are certain people easily found on the internet who have read the studies for you and provide a somewhat comprehensive bare-bones version of the combined results. The internet is full of misleading information as well, so make sure your source references the scientific studies where they derived their information from, and that they don't have biases towards certain information as they are trying to sell you something.

On that note, be extremely careful of any information that you read or is presented to you. Just because you see it online or in ten different articles, doesn't necessarily make it correct or correct for you. Be critical of all information, so critical that you even question the information I present to you in this book. Your life and your future depend on you making informed choices. Do your own research and try things out to see if they work for you. Question everything until you are happy with the answers.

Don't let this science talk bog you down. If certain medical conditions affect you or you have specific body goals, then go a little deeper on the information for your own well-being. If you're happy with some basics and don't know where to start, the following information will be a great beginning on your nutrition journey.

Let us simplify some of the big science-talk and address some of the basics.

There are three main sources of energy from food, these are from carbohydrates, fats, and proteins. These three are important to remember. While each of these can give you energy through different methods, they each have other impacts on other areas of your health (other than energy). To sustain a motivated life, we need energy, not only to focus but to achieve our goals physically. This doesn't mean consuming access amount of energy-producing foods because our body will then store them as fat. It means making sure that we always have enough energy from foods to meet our needs, and not more. We are no longer in an era where the body needs to store large amounts of fats to *survive the winter*, so to speak. But our genetic programming still wants to do this, hence why it can be, unfortunately, too easy to store fat for many people.

When you hear someone talk about macros (macronutrients), what they are talking about is the ratio between carbs, fats and proteins, our energy sources in your meals. Some people have very specific and measured macros for what they eat. Personally, I have never weight measured my carbs, proteins, and fats, but I have an understanding for roughly how they should look on my plate, and that is sufficient for me. Very few of us have time to be weighing our food. How boring and unmotivating that would be.

If I am trying to lose weight by losing fat, then my carbs will be the first thing to decrease. How would this look in the real world? I would eat less rice, pasta, bread, and sugars in each meal. If I were exercising two times per day, then I would increase my carbohydrates so that I could get immediate energy from them. Notice how sometimes I decrease carbs, and sometimes I increase carbs? That's because my goals change as does my needs. As a Pacific Islander I also need to factor in that genetically, Polynesians don't process carbohydrates as well as some other nationalities, and thus the increase in diabetes in our people. Your set of conditions and my set of conditions are different. What I will say is that the current western diet has us consuming an overabundance of carbohydrates. We find sugars in our bread. We consume too much bread and pasta, and we don't match our calorie intake to our activity level.

Everything has a price, and in this case, that price is weight gain. Our body stores those calories for what it considers a later date. In men, that storage happens mainly around the belly, and for women around the thighs, the reason for this is our hormonal structure differs between men and women.

* * *

Hunger

"Understanding your relationship with food will allow you to enjoy it in a manner that improves your health."

Growing up with many siblings and not much money for food was tough. But there were benefits. I could have grown up constantly battling with my siblings for the few pieces of meat we could afford for our family soup. But instead, I grew up learning how to share limited resources, and how to value food as a source of nutrition. As you read this chapter, think about your relationship with food, and what lessons in your life, whether right or wrong, stuck with you around food.

Competition for limited resources could have made me find ways to stuff myself with food during the times in which it was available, especially if we didn't know when the next meal was. Luckily, my parents had taught us the importance of looking after others and not just of ourselves. This meant that all food was shared equally, even if there wasn't much food to share. Sometimes we would still be hungry after meals, but we were never greedy.

The benefit of growing up on a farm was that despite not having store bought food we had the land. If we were still hungry, we could climb mango or coconut trees to get fruit. We would expend energy to get energy. Our self-discipline around not overconsuming food and sharing with others still serves me to this day.

We learned early to be able to stop eating. Had my parents not instilled the sharing mentality, then it could have been a whole different story, wherein we stuffed ourselves with food to get us through till the next meal. Sometimes we were hungry, but we were always disciplined.

Do you understand your relationship with food? Was there always an abundance or lack of food when you were growing up? What were some of the messages that you were told around nutrition? Did your parents tell you not to leave the table until your plate was finished? Think through these questions and get an understanding of what food was taught to mean to you. This isn't about having all the answers but just about finding your understanding and your thought blueprint around nutrition

When you start to feel hungry, that feeling is caused by two hormones:

1) Leptin

2) Ghrelin

I like to remember these two as being leprechauns and gremlins, two mythical little beings. The naughty gremlin (ghrelin) who travels from your empty stomach tells your brain that you are hungry. The well-dressed leprechaun (leptin) travels mainly from fat cells and tells your brain that you are full. I start here because hunger and our need for food is an extreme motivator. When we are hungry not only do we lack energy, but our mood is also affected, and we can end up hangry — a dangerous mix of hungry and angry! If our hormone leptin isn't being heard by our brain, while our hormone ghrelin is allowed to roam free, then we can overeat. It would be great to use our mental strength to fight these hormonal urges to over consume, but let's be honest, it would be even easier if they were functioning properly, so that we didn't need to be at war with ourselves.

So what goes wrong? Just because we have a lot of fat and thus leptin stores, it doesn't mean that our little leprechaun can get his message to our brain to tell it to stop eating. So what our body does is start a big loop. It believes we don't have enough stored fat because leptin can't get through to tell the brain that you are full. So it does two things. Firstly, it stores more fat from food, and secondly, it can decrease energy levels purposefully as it believes you don't have enough fat and, therefore, energy. It may purposefully limit your energy. See how this could affect motivation? This then starts a vicious cycle of fat gain and energy loss.

Are you starting to see how a simple hormone can play a profound effect on your energy and body composition? You are fighting an uphill battle if you are attempting to use only will power to beat fat loss and thus hunger issues. Whilst it is possible with extreme motivation to do this why not take on a two-way approach whereby, we increase our will power through training the habit of stopping just before we feel full and secondly, we look at maximizing how our body uses hormones to make an easier path for our willpower.

There are many theories on how to address leptin resistance, they include improving gut health, reducing inflammation, improving sleep etc. Most of these are dietary changes. It isn't by chance that people who eat nutritious based diets have better hormonal regulation in general. Decreasing sugar and excessive carbohydrate may also help by reducing triglycerides (fat) in the blood. This has a two-fold effect in that calories are decreased but so is Leptin resistance. Now we do need some fat for survival and for certain metabolic processes. You can measure your fat levels through calipers or by getting a DEXA (bone density or dual-energy x-ray absorption) scan. This will tell you exactly how much fat you have, where it is stored and what the healthy range should be.

There isn't a magic bullet for dealing with hunger. It is a powerful and necessary tool to help us survive. The problem is that we live in a time of abundant food and less than ideal self-control. Slow down your eating and enjoy the meal. Have smaller portions per serving. Allow leptin the leprechaun time to tell your brain that you are full and when this happens train your self-discipline muscle to listen. It may feel nice to get that extra food in, but at some stage, you will pay the price for over-consumption, it may not be today, but it will catch you.

* * *

Energy

"Having energy is a balancing act between what goes into your body and what activities you do to burn that energy. Your task is to find the balance."

Action taken from being motivated requires energy from nutrition. Too much food energy and we store it as fat, too little energy and we get tired whilst not being able to complete a task. In modern society, having too little energy from food is quite rare as opposed to over-consuming food. Having extra energy from food won't lead to increased motivation, but it will ensure that you are fueled to undertake the tasks that you seek motivation for.

When you hear someone talk about energy from food, they use the word calorie. A food calorie is technically known as a Kilocalorie. But we don't need to know this for our purposes, just be aware of it in case someone challenges your new-found knowledge.

Where this all gets confusing is that we talk about food in calories and the exercise machines in the gym also state calories burned, yet when we buy food in many parts of the world, it's common to see the energy content stated in kilojoules (kJ). What a great way to confuse us consumers and make us over consume. Luckily, I am here to make this conversion simpler.

Four kJ is roughly one food calorie.

If you purchase a loaf of bread, and it states that one slice has 400 kJ, then we divide that number by four, and we get a hundred calories in that slice of bread. We now walk over to our treadmill and go for a brisk walk. We may find that it takes us thirty minutes of walking to burn the energy from that slice of bread. Is it worth it? Maybe it is for some; perhaps it isn't for others. But at least we know.

The science of how we use fuel to make energy is quite complex and involves words like ATP and glucose. Simplifying it, we see that the cells of our body need energy from food to allow them to function.

There are four ways for us to burn energy in a day. You don't need to remember their names but get a grasp of how they work. They are:

BMR or Base Metabolic Rate – This is also loosely known as your metabolism. It is the energy we need just to maintain our weight while we spend the day doing nothing. Breathing, blinking, sleeping etc., uses energy. BMR can use roughly 60% of our daily energy expenditure.

NEAT – Non-exercise activity thermogenesis — This is the energy we burn when we go about our daily tasks. This could be chores, walking around our workplace, cooking dinner etc. It is called non-exercise activity because the purpose of it isn't to exercise but to do daily tasks. It makes up roughly 20% of our daily energy expenditure.

EAT – Exercise Activity Thermogenesis – This is the energy we burn when we train our body in exercise specific activity such as lifting weights or going for a walk. It constitutes roughly 10% of our energy use.

TEF – Thermic effect of food — The energy needed to digest the food you eat. The TEF depends on several factors including the type of food. Around 10% of our daily energy requirement comes from this digestive need.

What does this all mean? The biggest takeaway from it is that if we want to lose fat, then simple exercise alone (around 10%) makes it very hard to do so. What we want to do is maximize all areas of our energy expenditure. We need to be more active in general (less sedentary) to increase our non-exercise activity. We also need to find ways to increase our metabolism such as through building more lean muscle tissue.

The good news for those who struggle with exercise is that close to 80-90% of how our body looks is accomplished through simple non-exercise specific habits that we can do at home. Eating well and moving more just within our home and workplace will have a large effect on your body composition. The final 10-20% of your body shape will come from the sculpting process you do when you exercise either with weights, body weight or through sports and cardio.

So how does my plate look? When I was in my early twenties, it had a lot of carbohydrates because they were foods that made me full and happy but were also cheap. I had endless amounts of bread, potatoes, and rice. That worked well at the time because my activity level and hormone levels matched. Now if I want to lean-up, then sugars are the first thing to decrease. My dinner plate these days is full of nutritious steamed vegetables with small amounts of meat and very small amounts of carbohydrates. I consume a lot of fruit and vegetables, while I minimize dairy and processed or packaged foods. Is this right for everyone? Maybe, maybe not. It works for me, but you will need to find what works for you.

Every food item or chemical you consume will interact with your body in some way. If there are foods which you often eat, then have a rough understanding of what they do for you, and how many calories they have. For example, I enjoy having a banana in my morning smoothie, and I have for years. Because it is an item that I consume daily, I need to understand exactly what it does to my body. I know an average-sized banana has around a hundred calories and would take twenty to thirty minutes to walk off those calories. I also know that it has good levels of dietary fiber which helps digestion. There are too many foods for me to go through all of them, but the key here is to understand what impact your most commonly consumed foods have on you.

If you want to know what's happening internally, then getting blood tests is an excellent place to start. Blood is the river of life. It transports oxygen and nutrients to cells and removes by-products of metabolism and activity from cells. If you lack motivation, then it could be that you are lacking certain vitamins and the best way to see this is through blood testing. A good doctor or nutritionist can help you see exactly where you may be lacking. I've known people who were lacking in iron, B vitamins, and even vitamin D, who were constantly feeling lethargic. Some blood work and a readjustment of diet either through supplements or whole foods changed their motivation levels. They had more energy and mental clarity. Remember that there are safe ranges for certain vitamins. Don't over consume something just because you feel you are lacking. Everything in moderation.

Our brain hasn't completely evolved to deal with the amount of food most of us now have access to. We tend to overeat because it feels good. It is our genetics that tells us to overeat for fear of not knowing when there will be another meal. That's why food tastes so good, it gives us a feel-good reward in order to ensure we keep seeking more food so that we don't starve and die. For most of us, this is leading to over-consuming and health problems.

Be strict with yourself and understand that food is to help us survive and maximize life. Dig deeper to find what foods work for you and your genetic makeup. Make food about nutrition and not comfort and your health and motivation will change for the better.

Exercise

"One of the greatest forms of therapy is exercise. The body is made to move, and through targeted movement, we invite health."

Goal – The goal of this chapter is to highlight the importance of exercise in ensuring a motivated life. I then give simple yet effective principles you can use right away to improve your exercise habits.

Our body is made to move, not to be stagnant. Instead of thinking of exercise as isolated periods of movement, it is better to think of life as movement or rest. When it's time to sit at the computer and get work done, then you are in a state of physical rest (from exercise). When it's time to move, then you are exercising. While there should be periods of intense, structured exercise (gym, yoga, sports, etc.), it would benefit you to see any movement you do as an opportunity to become stronger and healthier. Your goal is to move more throughout your day as a whole.

Remember the saying, *use it, or lose it*. If we are able, daily, to use our body and put it through good healthy movement, then not only will we look and feel better, but our mind will function clearer. When we move from the idea that exercise is a chore to exercise is a privilege and an opportunity to grow, the whole game changes. Put music next to a child, and they instinctively move and dance, and so we must access our inner child that needs to move to the music of life.

I have been exercising and training my whole life. But I don't view training the same way most people do. It is never a chore, but a beautiful form of expression and self-love. I grew up on a farm with no exercise equipment other than a chin-up bar welded together from old fence posts. It was all we had. As kids, each day we would meet all the other kids from the nearby farmhouses and play communal sports. Every afternoon, without fail, it was as consistent as our attendance at school. Sometimes we would play rugby or touch or soccer, or we would all go for long walks and climb the mango trees at the far end of the farm. We would sit in them for hours, and then weave baskets from the leaves of coconut trees to carry our mangos back to our house. Each afternoon would be constant movement, and we were happy. Back then, video games had barely become mainstream, and we couldn't afford them anyway. Some days we would hitch-hike after school and be dropped off at the main road and have to walk four kilometers just to get home. As kids, we felt no loss from having to walk this far, and we grew up looking forward to our after-school sporting events on the farm. We grew up with a healthy love for movement. I look back now and see the positive association I have with exercise stemmed from my afternoons running back and forwards with the other kids.

Not everyone will be as lucky as I was to grow up on the expanses of a large farm, surrounded by nature. Many of you will have grown up either in the suburbs or cities. If your parents had put you in various sports or if you found ways to play with your friends, then you will most probably have a healthy love for exercise. If on the other hand, you grew up where exercise wasn't a thing, then this may have tainted your view of movement. Regardless of how or where you were raised, it is our job to rewire our brain to have a healthy love for exercise moving forward. We create this love by removing the self-imposed pressure of 'having to exercise' and replacing it with finding sports or activities that we can enjoy, whether communal or individual. Our goal is just to find things that allow us to move and feel good doing it. Walking the dog is exercise as is shooting hoops at the local basketball court. Working on your garden is exercise as is chasing after your child at the park.

Once you've courted your new love of movement, then, and only then, look at ways to start shaping your physique and training in a way that benefits your health and fitness goals.

Everyone reading this will have some exercise goals. These goals may range from being able to walk to the letterbox, to becoming an Olympic athlete. It would be wrong of us to look down on others' exercise goals based on our current standards of exercise. I have great respect for anyone who is trying to better themselves in any area of life. When I see someone struggling with weight loss, pushing themselves to exercise, I get the same inspiration as when I see an Olympic athlete pushing themselves to get stronger or faster. Unless we are in sporting competitions, then our results are not in comparison to others but only to our self of yesterday. Our goal with exercise is to improve on what we were yesterday and not on what other people are today. Remember that any step forward, no matter how small, is progress; and progress brings results. Results and growth bring happiness. And happiness within ourselves and those we care for is the ultimate measure of success.

Just as with nutrition there is a lot of conflicting information about how to exercise for optimum results.

The truth is that there are many ways to get to where you need to be. This said, there are general principles that work for everybody, but your exercise routine will depend entirely on your goals.

My exercise routine constantly changes because my situation and goals change. As a multi-sport Olympian, this is challenging at times as each sport requires a different physique. When I went from Taekwondo to cross-country skiing my training had to change as did my goals and my body shape. This was made easier because I had a strong exercise foundation. I already loved movement because of my childhood and my body was primed to be efficient at whatever I decided to put it through. If your goal is to lose fat and get more muscle tone, then you have an advantage over me in that your goal is one tracked. You don't need to lose muscle for one sport and put on muscle for another. Just because you didn't grow up running on a farm doesn't mean you don't have advantages that can benefit you. Focus in on that goal.

The body is a master of efficiency. It wants to minimize energy expenditure whilst still doing the same task that you put it through. If you decide to run long distances every day, it will be hard at the start but as your body adapts it will become easier. Your body will find ways to make the same task as energy efficient as possible. This is a double-edged sword.

On the one hand, we get more efficient, and the task becomes easier. And on the other, the body adapts, and we hit exercise and motivation plateaus. Plateaus are where we train really long and hard and yet fail to see the results of our effort. The body has adapted. To break through that plateau, we also need to adjust our training methods. We do this by either cycling different training programs or through progressive overload. Progressive overload is where we slowly increase the intensity of the exercise. We can increase intensity by increasing duration, speed, weight, etc., of the practice. We may even decrease the time taken to do a training session but also decrease the rest time between sets of exercise. We want to safely overload our muscles, and thus force them to grow and adapt to the new and more challenging workout.

So how does this look in the real world? Let's take someone looking to lose fat and build muscle. I use this example as it is the most common goal from an exercise perspective even more so than to improve health. Society has unfortunately become shallow, but that's a story for another day. I digress. Putting diet aside, we would need to do two things to lose fat and build muscle.

Progressively and safely overload the muscles with weight training to build body shape. Engage in some form of cardio to lose fat.

By lifting weights whether at the gym or body weight at home you will also be burning fat. Cardio could be walking the dog, running on a treadmill, or doing High-Intensity Interval Training (HIIT). Cardio as we know it comes in two simple forms. You can jog or move in some way slowly over say an hour, or you can do sprinting exercises over a shorter period, i.e. HIIT. The basic science is that you will burn fat while you jog slowly, and you will burn fat while you sprint. The difference is that sprinting will result in you burning fat even after you stop the action of sprinting. All the exertion makes your body go into hyperdrive and continue to burn calories for hours after the session, assuming the intensity was high enough. This is great for losing body fat, but there is a downside. HIIT is a whole lot less fun than, say, walking your dog. The sessions are shorter. Still, they result in you gasping for breath and wondering why you ever started.

If your current health isn't up to the task, then you will need to work into HIIT training under professional guidance as the intensity is very high. You will also find that doing HIIT more than two to three times a week can be demotivating because of the exertion level and may have a diminishing result as your body doesn't heal in time between sessions.

So do you walk the dog or do HIIT? I'm glad you asked! Do what you can consistently do week in and week out. HIIT will get you quick results but if you end up in pain or having a negative association with exercise then go back to walking the dog daily so to speak. If you are an exercise beast, then do both.

In training for the Summer Olympics in Taekwondo, I was doing a Taekwondo form of HIIT every day. This involved intense kicking on a bag for twenty seconds followed by a minute's rest and I did this for thirty minutes. The results were incredible, I lost a lot of fat and got faster, well that is until I not only got injured but I started to hate it. Hating exercise is a red flag and injury is an even bigger red flag. Even Olympians can hit moments when they hate training. When this happens, it's time for a rest session. Everything in moderation and everything should be balanced. Find the balance that works for you between walking the dog and doing some form of interval training. Find a coach that is experienced in this and your results will come.

Now back to lifting weights. If you've hit a physical and motivational plateau, then you need to change either your intensity, your consistency, or your program. That's all there is to it.

Consistency — This is the most crucial aspect in my opinion. If I gave someone three hours total to exercise per week, they would most probably choose to do three sessions of one hour. I would much prefer that instead of this they did six sessions of thirty minutes. Why? Because consistency is critical if you want results with exercise. You would be surprised at what you can get done in thirty minutes. Training three times a week and expecting big results just won't happen in an acceptable amount of time. Professional athletes, the ones that we look up to live and breathe exercise. Your thirty minutes a day of targeted exercise is easily achievable. I am sure you spend more time than that scrolling through your social media news feed every day. Invest in yourself through consistency.

Intensity — This is the second most crucial element in overcoming an exercise plateau. Intensity doesn't mean training longer; it means training harder while remaining safe. I say safe because the risk of injury is very real when you train hard. We want to avoid any damage at all costs. Intensity could mean adding more weight, shortening the rest time between sets or just pushing harder in each set. The simple way I measure intensity is sweat. If someone isn't sweating in the gym, then that's the first sign to me of low intensity. Yes, some people sweat less, but I'm always looking out for it when helping people train. But what if the air conditioning is on? It really doesn't matter. As a cross country skier, we would go into sub-zero, freezing conditions in nothing but unflattering superhero looking lycra and still come back covered in sweat. You want results? Then you need to get comfortable with sweat. This is a gym and not a night out on the town. Your focus should be on your results.

Many people are worried about overtraining, yet the majority of people I see are mostly undertraining. If you want to know what over-training intensity looks like, join a Muay Thai gym in Thailand and do four to six hours a day in the blistering heat, while getting hit by dedicated trainers. I would do this once a year every year just to remind myself what real intensity looks like. I got great results very quickly, but it wasn't sustainable in the long run due to the intensity and injury potential. My Thailand training camps never lasted more than one month while doing three sessions a day. So long as the body recovers well, and you aren't getting injured, then you probably aren't overtraining.

Program — If you're stuck in a training plateau, then the last thing to look at is your training program. If you've been doing the exact same program for the last year, your body has probably found a way to adapt. Remember it doesn't necessarily want to build muscle unless it has to. Muscle uses energy by increasing your metabolic rate, and the body wants to conserve energy. We can change our training program in a few ways. We can add more weight, or we can add or decrease rest time. We can do super-sets, or we can do drop sets. Or we can change our whole exercise program every couple of months. While your program is important, I do believe that the majority of people who seek expert advice will find decent enough programs. To beat the plateau, you will need to ensure your program changes regularly every couple of months or so. Now, some exercises will be the base of any program and won't change, and so you can keep those in but change how they're done and what other activities are in the program with them.

When I walk through a gym, I see people with complex programs with far too many exercises. Unless you're a professional bodybuilder trying to increase the short head of the bicep, then ask your trainer to keep your program simple. Motivation is about simplifying everything to a point where you don't need to think. I average four different exercises per session in the gym. If I feel a boost of extra power, I might hit six just for fun with the last two being extra but not necessary. Any more than six, and I get confused and unmotivated. Keep it simple, and you will keep doing it.

Start your exercise motivation with small movements and small habits. Build them up as your willpower strengthens. If you can't do twenty minutes of exercise a day, then do five minutes. If you can't do five minutes, then do one minute. Your goal is to build a habit and increase time doing it from there. The New Year's resolution to get in shape doesn't need you to join a gym and do an hour every day in January. This is why most people fail by February, too much too soon. You have to grow your motivation by starting as small as you can consistently manage, then progressively do more and more.

If you're a professional sportsperson, you probably already know a lot of the meat of this section. That said, the fundamentals are the same. If you want to get better at a sport, then you need to go back to basics. Perfect the basics, and then progressively do more. I can't stress working with the basics enough. I have seen Olympic Taekwondo athletes win Gold medals with nothing more than a perfect roundhouse kick while their opponents would do elaborate spinning kicks in the air. One kick to Gold. A professional athlete can spend hours per day training. Over time, this can become monotonous. Just remember that as soon as training stops being fun, your results will suffer. Find ways to maintain intensity while keeping your training both simple and fun.

Most people over-complicate their exercise. They think they need gyms and fancy equipment to get results. Yes, these things are nice, but they certainly aren't necessary. The majority of my exercise is at home. I grew up using crude equipment but always got results. You don't need a perfect set of circumstances to do exercise. If you're at home cooking, then you can do bodyweight squats while waiting for food to cook. If you're too tired to go to the gym, then you can do a hundred push-ups at home and call it a chest session. If you're a stay at home mom, then you can lay on your back and high five your young daughter as you do twenty minutes with sets of crunches. Remember that consistency is the most essential part of exercise. Just do something. Whatever you can do, do that. As your situation and motivation for exercise changes, then you can go to the gym or to that Pilates class.

Don't let the lack of a perfect set of circumstances stop you from achieving the results you want. Your life and your physical and mental well-being rely on you to make use of any free time to exercise. Allow yourself to fall in love again with what your body was born to do, move.

8-Step Motivation Guide

"Motivation is about two things; Dealing with inner conflict and creating great habits. Work on both, and you will win in life."

We have gone on an interesting journey to understand the various elements of motivation. Some of you may even have found some piece of knowledge that you can use right away to help you. In the following pages, I will be presenting the eight steps that you can apply immediately into your life to help you as you go on your motivation journey. The previous sections taught you about building a foundation and understanding the mechanics of motivation. They showed you what goes wrong and what challenges we face when trying to get motivated. Following are eight steps that I apply to my own life and that have created massive changes in my ability to complete tasks and achieve seemingly impossible dreams. Your new-found knowledge will arm you with an understanding of the psychology of motivation, and how you can apply it to improve every area of your life. They say knowledge opens doors. So let's continue.

Step 1 — Write Down Your Goals

"The biggest mistake in goal setting is to set 'realistic goals.' Your true potential doesn't lie in the easily achievable but in the perceived impossible."

Yep, you read that right. Setting realistic dreams and overarching goals is a mistake I see all too often. Realistic sub-goals can help, but your dream is also your ceiling. You don't want a ceiling to cap your potential. Your potential is limitless, but more about that later.

The first step in any journey is knowing where it is that you want to go. From there, you can work backwards and fill in the details. In fact, I don't worry about the details or the plan until long after I am already on the road towards the goal. Planning is crucial, but if we over plan, then we risk never starting — also known as *analysis paralysis*. We analyze something so much that we never actually do it.

A goal is nothing more than a clear destination that you want to get to. Imagine starting a hundred-meter sprint race with an invisible finish line. While some may accidentally bumble their way across, most of us will never reach it. We would end up in the stadium, running backwards, or even colliding with each other. Now imagine if that finish line was clearly set out and there were lanes for you to follow as is the case in most sprint races. Your efficiency and speed to crossing the finish line would be near an optimal level. And even if you were a slow runner, you would at least know that you were heading in the right direction at your best speed. That in itself is motivating. The finish line represents the goal, and the lanes represent the quickest path to that goal.

Now if we took our hundred-meter sprint race and turned it into a forty-two-kilometer marathon, things change for the worse. Without a clear direction or destination, how far we end up away from where we want to be would be greatly magnified. One degree in the wrong direction at the start can put us even further off course down the track. This marathon represents many of life's longer-term goals. Now there is always the benefit of correcting your course if you find yourself off track. And many a time we will have to do this. But a simple, small step at the beginning of a journey will save you a lot of pain and work further on that journey. Writing down that goal is this first step. You can follow this goal with a rough plan to get there. But the goal always comes first.

I could never understand why writing down a goal could help achieve that goal. As an engineer, I was overly logical and just couldn't conceptualize the difference between writing down a goal and having a goal in my head. At that stage, I hadn't yet made an Olympic Games and was doing relatively okay at life. By okay, I mean I was in the rat race getting average results but still working hard. Eventually, it all made sense after I decided to write down my goals. Once I did this, I saw the results, and to this day I am a goal setting believer.

For the majority of us mere mortals, having a goal in our head is like having an imaginary finish line. It only exists in the realm of thought. The problem is that the goals we want to achieve need to exist in the real world; the World that we can see and hear and touch. If we want that car, health, or happiness we want it not just in dreams but here in front of us. Writing down a goal is the first and most important step in achieving it. Why? Because it is us taking an idea out of our mind and manifesting it in a real, tangible form. We can see it, we can touch it, and we can do so whenever we please. By doing this, we are inviting our goal into the real world.

There are many ways to write down a goal statement. The simplest is that we write down what it is that we want to achieve, and then we follow it up with a date as to when we want to achieve it. A goal without a date is nothing more than a dream or a thought. The chapter on procrastination showed why this date is so important. A date adds an element of completion pressure and forces you to work harder in order to achieve it.

I never wrote down my goals growing up. As I mentioned earlier, I thought it was sufficient to have a goal in my head. The problem with a goal residing in the mind is that it comes and goes depending on your mood or your focus. A goal written down stays in front of you and reminds you to get it done. It is not influenced by the weather or the seasons or your mood or the challenges you face. It is unwavering just like your conviction should be in achieving it. You can mentally justify why you can avoid and rest from chasing that goal in your mind, but you can't mentally remove a very real piece of paper with your goal written on it. To do so would require a physical action which is harder to do than to lie to ourselves about how we can have a day off from chasing down our goals.

I remember one cool, spring day in Seoul, Korea. I had been living in a preschool for six months sleeping underneath a desk as the preschool belonged to the church and they allowed me to stay. The caveat was that each morning at five a.m., I would need to pack up my bags and be out for the day, while the kids came in for their schooling. This particular day, my coach, Master Paul, was with me and suggested we go to the Kukkiwon museum. The Kukkiwon is the center of Taekwondo. It is like the temple that all Taekwondo players should visit at some time in their life. We caught a one-hour train there and proceeded to explore the museum. Something clicked in me that day. I was feeling strangely inspired and strong after seeing years of Taekwondo history right there in front of me. At this

The Motivation Station

stage, I was preparing for the London Olympic qualifier, after missing out four years earlier. As we left, I noticed a large guest book sitting on one of the glass displays. I stopped my coach and proceeded to write in the book.

"Pita Taufatofua, Taekwondo Tonga, Future Olympian, May 18th 2011"

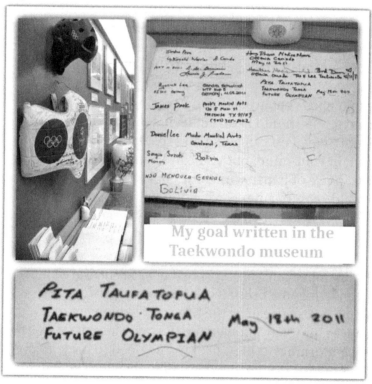

I took a photo and left. I looked at that photo at least once a week for the next few years. Two months later, I just missed out on my second Olympic qualifier after an injury at the World Championships left me with a torn knee ligament. And five years later, that goal that I had written down on that chilly spring day came true. I had invited it into the world, and still to this day, it stands in the Kukkiwon museum, forever part of history.

By the time I decided to go for my second Olympics, I was extremely proficient at writing goals. I wrote down *To qualify for the Winter Olympics within one year in a new sport.* I then took up cross country skiing, a sport I had never done before, and put skis on for the first time in my life; my goal was clear — largely impossible, but very clear. I wanted to qualify in a sport that I had no head-starts in. I wasn't an endurance athlete. I only experienced snow a few years earlier, but I wanted to prove to myself and to others just what they could be capable of if they really wanted to achieve their goals. I worked day and night for a whole year, sacrificing many lucrative options that had come up from my exposure at the Summer Olympics.

My finances had dried up, and I couldn't work as I had to train all day every day to be able to qualify within a year. On top of that, I was working on a relationship with a girl I had known for many years and whom I loved. That relationship became strained because of my position and dedication to my Olympic Journey. I lost a lot in that year. Unknown to the world, I had hit rock bottom.

But something never changed, the fire inside me only grew stronger as my challenges grew harder. My purpose, the Olympic Dream, and my quest to show people what they are capable of achieving kept calling me through the pain and struggle. I had to work hard to get the reward. A few days short of one year later, I qualified for my second Olympics in a sport I had never done in a climate and event I wasn't built for. There is power in writing down your goals.

A goal statement says what it is that you want to achieve and by when. When I first wrote my goal statement in the Kukkiwon, I didn't have an exact date, but I did have the word *future*. I was new to goal statements at that time. Perhaps this is why I missed out two months later, or maybe it needed more time to manifest. I will never know, but it worked, and still to this day, I make a habit of writing down all my goals.

An example of a goal statement might be *I want to earn a million dollars within five years,* or *I want to eat a healthy diet rich in vegetables from now on.* It could be *I want to own my own company within three years,* or *To feel healthy and happy every single day.*

What are some of your goals? When do you want to achieve them by? Let's get to work and write them down. There is no right or wrong way, and a goal can be amended. For now, let's just bring them out of our mind and into a tangible written form. Put down this book and find the first piece of paper you can and write them down. You can transfer them to something more solid later, or you can stick that napkin or receipt on your fridge indefinitely. Just get it done and do it now.

* * *

Welcome back. There are ways to make your goal statement even more powerful. One of these ways is to create a vision board. A vision board is basically a cork board with pictures of what it is that you want out of life, things that inspire you. You should hang it up in a place where you can view it throughout the day. A picture is worth a thousand words and people are visual creatures. Pictures can elicit emotions which can be more powerful than words alone. One of my personal goals is to see the Aurora Borealis with someone special. The Aurora is the beautiful Northern Lights that put on a show in the night sky a few times a year. The emotional reaction I get by seeing a picture of it is far more intense and motivating than a description of *See the Northern lights in the sky.*

Now if you pair your goal statement with visuals of your goals, you create a very compelling and motivational tool. The only reason I haven't seen the Aurora Borealis at this time is that I have purposefully delayed it. It is a goal that I would like to share with the right person and at the right time. Just because a goal is achievable immediately doesn't necessarily mean you have to, or even want to, achieve it immediately. It's nice to look out into the sky and dream. There are both power and comfort in knowing what good things lie ahead of you.

How a goal statement or vision board looks depends on the individual. Some people may prefer a vision book or a simple photograph that they can carry with them. If you grew up watching war movies, you would have seen that a lot of soldiers would carry pictures of their wife or kids. This simple picture would motivate and give them hope that they would soon see them again. Now sometimes life has its own plans, and not all soldiers would return to their families. But having that photograph gave them a clearer picture of direction, reason and made them *feel better*. The better someone feels, the easier it is for them to make good, clear decisions. Have you experienced a time where everything just felt good, which invited more good things? On the flip side have you ever had something go wrong which led to many more things going wrong? This vision board isn't a guarantee of success, but it certainly does heavily sway the cards in your favor.

Luck is nothing more than having something positive happen to you because you did things to increase the possibility of those things happening. It's a game of percentages and not just of chance. It makes sense that we would want to put all the cards in our favor.

Now there is a small percentage of people who have never written down their goals and yet achieved great things. For some people, the visuals are so burnt into their mind that it forms somewhat of an internal vision board. But generally speaking, these aren't the kinds of people that need help in attaining motivation. Unlike you and I, they may have been born with or had something happen to them that gave them a stronger, compelling direction that got them to where they needed to be. Now imagine if they did write down their goals or create a vision board, they might have achieved these things even earlier.

It isn't a good idea to take an outlier or 'extraordinary' person and say I will do it how they did it. Remember that each person is born with a unique set of gifts, talents, and life challenges. We can't exactly copy someone else's natural talents, but we can work hard at developing our own. We can follow mentors who have been successful, but even then, we would need to adapt their methods to suit our own strengths and weaknesses. In saying this even the knowledge, I present to you should be utilized in a way that works for you. Don't copy me in order to get my results. Instead, use the tools and stories I present to develop your own way of becoming motivated. This will be more sustainable for you in the long run.

A lot of the most successful people in the World have clear, defined goals and use tools that suit their individual style. They are clear in their intent and strong in their conviction. There is no right or wrong way to do this so long as you state your goal, give it a timeline, and make it visual. Vision plays into our emotions. Emotions are what drive us to take action. Action gives us progress, and progress makes us happy.

Writing a goal isn't enough. We must revise our goals daily or weekly. They must always stay in the forefront of our mind, like anything in life. Use it or lose it. If we stopped exercising, we would lose our strength and fitness. If we stopped setting money aside, our savings would eventually dry up. And if we stop revising our goals, then they too would disappear.

Do not be scared of seemingly impossible goals. Dream as big as you can imagine. I have said it a thousand times throughout my life, and I will say it a thousand more. People are constantly told to set realistic goals; this is a mistake. They write down things that do not strongly appeal to their inner desire. To get motivated to do something of value, it should be extremely appealing. Goals, dreams, and miracles happen every day. Believe that the dreams you have been given have also been given to you with the ability to achieve them. If someone anywhere in history with a similar physical make-up has been able to achieve it, why can't you? And if they haven't, then be the first.

Seemingly impossible dreams are more likely to happen when we first believe that they can. And they are so much more motivating than *realistic* half-dreams. The reason I have accomplished seemingly impossible things in a short amount of time isn't because I am particularly talented but because I have no fear when it comes to setting Impossible goals. If my mind can conceive it, and it excites me to chase it, then that is what I will do. If there are things that I fall short on, then I can say I had a blast and learned many lessons getting there. After all, isn't this adventure and pursuit of great challenges and self-growth a purpose of life? It sure is! It's like the saying, "Shoot for the moon, and if you miss, you still land amongst the stars."

One of the real reasons people don't set seemingly impossible goals is because they fear failing. Or said another way, they fear how they would think of themselves or what others would think of them if they failed. What if you were impervious to failure? What if you had failed so many times that it no longer pained you to fail? Some people would be demotivated and quit whilst many of you would be so unafraid to set big goals that you would fail your way to achieving them. You would be immune to people's opinions to the point that you would no longer value their negative criticisms of you. Write down that impossible dream and give it a date to make it a goal. Write down those things that your mind wanders to throughout the day. Where are you now and where are you meant to be? Either you write down the goals of your life or, in an often-unfair way, life will write them for you. Dream without limits.

Step 2 — Define Your Reasons

"A motivated life requires motivating reasons."

Every one of us has reasons as to why we want to do something. Your biggest source of motivation will come from your *why*. This is your reason for wanting to do or complete a task. Why is it that you want to achieve those goals from your goal statements? It will take a lot of work and sacrifice. It would be easier not to achieve them and continue staying in your current comfort zone. Why do you even want to be motivated in the first place? Is it because it's a buzz word and others are trying it, or is it because something inside you longs for more?

Our *why*, also known as our reason, dictates our outcome. Take exercise as an example. How often do you see people working hard at the gym when there is an important body-based deadline for them? This could be something as simple as to *look good for a European holiday* or *to be as fit as possible for an upcoming triathlon*. Summer could be just around the corner, and people want their best beach body. Right or wrong, we as humans often tie our feelings of happiness into events and what we think others will think of us during or after those events. This is why celebrities spend thousands of dollars for a single evening appearance at a red-carpet event. It is also why men and women will literally starve themselves to look their best at a particular time even though this negatively affects them in the long run.

If you ask someone why they want a six pack of abs, they will often say *to look good*. The underlying truth is not just to look good, but in their subconscious mind, it is to have others admire and value them because this would give them a feeling of significance, thus making them feel happy. If people were put on a deserted island where no one would ever see their six pack, I can almost guarantee that, all of a sudden, its importance would massively diminish. People want other people's admiration; it makes them feel good. Whilst there is nothing inherently wrong with this, it is a tool that we can leverage to motivate ourselves. Ultimately, validation should come from inside oneself, but for now, we find as many ways as possible to sustain our motivation; we use them to our advantage.

How was it possible to go from complete amateur to Olympic level skier in just one year? The short answer is motivation. Looking at the definition of motivation we see that it is: *a reason to do something*. What reasons could I possibly have given myself that would pull me up out of bed in the early hours of the morning to train up to six-hour days, day in and day out, for a year? What reasons would I need to drive thirty hours each way, just to get to a ski race on the other side of the Australian continent, or fly to fifteen countries in two months to pursue qualification races?

What if I told you that I created my reasons to be so compelling that I had no choice but to qualify. That the whole direction of my life depended on my ability to do the impossible. What if I then said that not only did I create reasons so compelling, but I publicly announced what I would do a year before doing it? I started by choosing an extremely challenging task, and then I also added pressure to myself by making it public. In my head, my whole future depended on whether I would qualify for the second Olympics or not. Whether this was the case is irrelevant, I had to believe it was. If I did qualify, there would be an abundance of opportunities for me to further improve my life by helping others around the world.

I had no choice but to make this a reality, people were relying on me. My motivating reason was to set an impossible goal and then to show people that they too could set impossible goals. I could not fail; it wasn't an option.

It is vital on your motivation journey to break down these reasons to their base emotion, the genuine reason we want to do something. Humans are complex creatures but what is known is that by leveraging raw emotions we will be able to achieve great things. If you keep asking yourself why you want to achieve something you will get to your raw emotion. Take for example my goal to qualify for the Winter Olympics. Why did I want to qualify for the Winter Olympics? To show the world that they can achieve their dreams. Why do I want to show the world that they can achieve their dreams? Because it would make me feel that I was contributing back to the people and the planet. Why do you want to contribute back to people and the planet? Because it would make me feel fulfilled that I was moving towards my purpose. Why do you want to feel fulfilled and move towards your purpose? Because it would make me feel happy and happiness and purpose is the reason, I believe I am on this planet. By asking enough why questions I was able to break down my goal to a base emotion, happiness, and purpose. Try this exercise and see where you get to. There is no right or wrong answer so long as you are honest with yourself.

Many a time I have heard people who are on an exercise and fitness journey state that their *why* is because they want to get fit. Why would *I want to get fit*, more often than not, result in poor outcomes? The reason is simple. *I want to get fit* doesn't elicit any strong emotional response. What does saying, "I want to get fit," even mean? As a two-sport Olympian, I still find that statement extremely vague and that it carries no clear meaning. Without a strong emotional response, it becomes a demotivating and vague *why statement*. Now if, on the other hand, their *why statement* became, "I want to improve my strength, speed, flexibility, and endurance, so that I am able to play with my kids and thus improve our quality of life, so that I can live longer and create great, happy memories with them," wouldn't that be a much stronger statement? They would then be tying their results in with the happiness outcomes of their children and their longevity on this planet (an intrinsic and primal motivator) which would lead to stronger long-term motivation.

Now let's take a financial *why statement*. A lot of people when asked what their financial *why statement* is, would say, "I want to be rich so that I can buy what I want." There is nothing wrong with wanting to be rich but placing it in such a statement as above will again elicit no strong emotional response. To achieve a difficult and rewarding outcome from life, we need to apply work. The only thing that is going to get us to do that work is a strong emotional and motivating reason. Why would anyone work if there was no strong reason to work? Now the above statement could be changed to, "I want to be wealthy so that I can provide my family and me with a lifestyle giving us options to do the things that we love. I want to remove the stresses of bills thus increasing our health and well-being. That would make me happy." This could be a much more powerful *why statement*.

For many, just to get through the day to day struggles of life requires an income, and so people take up a job. This seems to be a sufficient *why* according to their goal — to pay the bills and survive life to enjoy it after retirement. The danger here is that 99% of people are doing just that, surviving. We, on the other hand, don't just want to survive; we want to thrive. In order for this to happen, we need a *why statement* ingrained in us that is exciting, and again, emotion provoking. I cannot stress that enough. Emotion is a lasso that helps you harness motivation; use it.

On a personal level, I had an extremely emotion provoking *why statement* to be financially successful. I wanted to be able to, "Be wealthy so that I could purchase Mother a new set of teeth, so that she wasn't embarrassed to smile in photos. Seeing her smile would make me happy." While this may seem trivial to some, it was extremely emotionally motivating for me. My mother never smiled in photographs because she didn't like her teeth. These *why statements* are about you and what creates that strong motivating feeling within you. Helping my family feel happy does that for me.

Now I had a personal conflict with my goal and financial *why statement*. I grew up in a poor family with parents who told me that money isn't everything. They were right. But I took it a step further and decided that money wasn't important. I learned to be happy with not much, and this is a great thing to have. The problem was, I had parental messaging ingrained in me since childhood that gave me a very neutral or somewhat subconscious dislike of money. The inner conflict was that I wanted more to help people, but I kept telling myself, even as an adult, that I could be happy without it. And I was right, I was happy without it, but I also had placed a ceiling on how much of it I could get.

The problem was that the goals and dreams I had created were so big that I wanted and needed more money in order to achieve them. How was I going to build free gyms in the poor Pacific countries with no financing? How was I going to buy my mother a new set of teeth with nothing but happiness? I wasn't. And so my journey became one of changing the financial messaging that I had imprinted in myself my whole life.

Once I was able to do this, opportunities came in abundance. Each of you will have to understand your inner voice. Look for messages that conflict with your goals and find ways to change that voice to be more conducive to achieving your dreams. One of the ways to do this is with the raging wolf technique or with affirmations. Always start your *why statement* as though you are asking yourself a question and then answering that question back to yourself.

For example:

Why do you want to be successful in business? I want to be successful in business because it will provide me with an income and life experiences, such as travel, that will bring joy to myself and my family every single day.

The *why statement* is not a Goal Statement. We do not need a timeline or a plan; all we need is a strong motivating reason why we want to achieve our goals. This *why statement* is your go-to each time you revisit your goals or each time you feel your motivation is lacking. What are your *why statements*? What would compel you to take action towards your goals daily? Write them down and revise them often. Once your goal, and reason for it, is ingrained in you, then start formulating a plan. Don't get so caught up in a perfect plan that you lose sight of your goals.

Step 3 — Start Each Day with Gratitude

"A grateful mind is a happy mind."

There are two things that you should start each day with. They are achievement and gratitude.

Have you ever wondered why the tides work or a compass always points north? Before I talk about Gratitude, I want to talk about the mechanics behind positivity and some of the mysteries of the universe. This section will require you to think with an open mind.

As a young fourteen-year-old boy, I loved fishing. I couldn't get enough of it. I would run away from school to find fishing spots and would stay up all night without a single bite but was still very content. One Christmas, I travelled to the outer islands of Tonga to help our family put on a family feast. In those years, I didn't know what gratitude was, and I didn't really care.

One morning I asked my Uncle Hame if he could take me trawling. A type of fishing where we pull fishing lures behind the boat. I had the expectation that he would say yes; why wouldn't he? His selfish nephew was asking! I was so caught up in my goal of going fishing that I didn't realize what sacrifice my uncle would make to take me. He used his last few dollars to buy me fishing lures and to fill the petrol tank of a boat we borrowed from the neighbors. The seas were starting to get rough as a cyclone was forecast to hit the next day. I was so persistent that I didn't see the sacrifice my own family was making to facilitate my fishing trip. We got out into the ocean, and before long the weather had turned so bad that the waves were throwing our little boat around dangerously. We could only see land between the waves; they were that high. My cousin who was driving the boat started to get scared and headed directly back home. This was a mistake because the waves could have flipped the boat, if we didn't angle it to return on a different course. Uncle Hame, being an old seafarer, took control of the outboard motor and with his whole body shaking, slowly took us home to safety. My uncle had Parkinson's disease which left him without full motor control of his muscles.

I had been so focused on my goals and expected everything to happen for me that I couldn't see the stress that I was causing. In those early years, I didn't understand gratitude and its importance in life. My uncle passed away not long afterwards from his Parkinson's disease. He had given everything he had to improve my life, and I didn't give him the gratitude he deserved. I learned a lot from that day before the cyclone. And to this day, I am thankful and happy for the smallest of things.

My uncle Hame not long before he passed away from complications due to Parkinsons Disease.

My father is a scientist, and I received my university degree in engineering. I grew up with two schools of thought, one was religious, and one was scientific. Despite attending church every Sunday, I found that there was a part of me that was constantly critical, not just of religion and spirituality but of everything. I wasn't content being told information without a valid and vigorous explanation that could prove that information correct. It was in my DNA to question everything.

My grandfather on my mother's side had no belief in religion but was an extremely well-respected scientist and engineer. His mannerisms reminded me of a young Albert Einstein. He would shut himself in his office and design and tinker with transistor radios. I believe that I inherited DNA traits from him and my scientific/religious father that had me questioning everything. I felt utterly naked if someone challenged me on something I had said, and I didn't have a valid explanation for why I said it. I hated that feeling; so I studied everything I could about anything.

The more I studied, the more I found that there were huge gaps in our current knowledge of the Universe. This was tough for me to swallow because I needed answers, yet my questions had reached the cutting edge of science and understanding. I found that this frontier of science blurred with philosophy. And the more they intertwined, the stronger was my realization that philosophy and science were two sides of the same coin. We had to ask tough philosophical questions in order to progress with science and our understanding.

I eventually came to an essential and ground-breaking realization that would change my life. I found that I didn't have to understand the science behind everything; I only had to observe that there were things that would happen for which we couldn't yet understand *how*. Whilst I will continue to seek answers to some of life's most significant questions, I am content with not knowing until the time that that information reveals itself to me. What this meant was that I could take an observation and turn it into something useful that could immediately benefit my life. I didn't have to know what caused the wind, but I could harness its strength to help me sail across the seas.

The laws of the universe are complex in how they work but simple in what they do. From the outset, we will state that we don't yet know the exact science behind them, but we are able to observe them at different times. Remember science is nothing more than us being able to reproduce the results of an experiment with consistency and measure these results. Until we knew the Gravitational Formula linking any object in the universe with any other universal object, we didn't know exactly how one physical object could influence another physical object. Yet we were able to observe ocean tides. What we later found out was that the mass of the moon would pull on the oceans of the earth causing these tides.

The science came long after humans were able to observe the effects. There was a force at play (gravity) that we couldn't see, but we could watch what it did. Now that we have a formula for it, we call it science.

The truth is we don't really know why or how this invisible force exists. Another example of an invisible force is that of magnetic force. The magnetic force is the reason a lot of electronics can function. For hundreds of years, we observed compass needles pointing north but could not scientifically understand the reason. What if there were more forces currently beyond our understanding, forces where we could observe their effects but didn't quite understand? Meet gratitude and positivity.

Have you ever noticed that certain people are constantly barraged with negative experiences and outcomes whereas others always seem to be 'lucky' in life? In many major religions or spiritual practices, we see common threads of texts, and from completely unrelated sources, about cause and effect.

From a Biblical standpoint, we have the verse from the book of Matthew 7:12: "do unto others as you would like done unto you." Does this statement mean that if we do good to others, something good will happen to us? And if so, how do we even measure or link such things?

Whilst you may not be religious, what you will find is that such a statement of cause and effect appears in many places in both religious and non-religious text. If you look at the following examples you will see some of these;

In Buddhist and Hindu teachings, they speak about Karma. Karma is the principle that what you do comes back to you in some later form. It is a cornerstone of cause and effect.

"As you think so shall you become" – By the late Bruce Lee

"As you sow so shall you reap" – Galatians 6

"There are no accidents in my philosophy. Every effect must have its cause. The past is the cause of the present, and the present will be the cause of the future. All these are links in the endless chain stretching from the finite to the infinite." – Abraham Lincoln

"Everything happens for a reason." – Commonly quoted saying

"There isn't smoke without fire." – French saying

"Shallow men believe in luck; strong men believe in cause and effect." – Ralph Waldo Emerson

"Scientific research can reduce superstition by encouraging people to think and view things in terms of cause and effect." – Albert Einstein

We could go on and on with a myriad of examples about cause and effect from entirely different and unrelated sources, but I think you get the idea.

So why is it that there are so many interpretations on the same thing and all from independent sources? If we take the frame that there must be some or a lot of truth in these teachings, then we open ourselves to vast possibilities and opportunities that are beyond our scope of understanding. We don't have to know how the Universe works we just have to understand that it does and that we can draw beneficial outcomes from it.

I'll get back to gratitude. Gratitude is a feeling of being appreciative and grateful in life. It is the thought we have in our head that puts a positive feeling just on waking up each day. So why is gratitude so important in the context of motivation? With our new knowledge of how the universe works, karma and cause and effect we see that by expressing positivity and appreciation we are in essence saying "thank you" to the universe. What happens when you say thank you to someone? Are they more or less likely to want to help you out in the future? You've got it, much more likely. So by being grateful to God or the Universe, you are inviting positive things to enter into your life.

This may sound like a selfish thing to do. But it's quite the contrary. There is so much pain and hate and negativity in this world, that by being grateful, we are creating positivity to balance the yin and yang of the universe. We do it because it is a win-win situation. We are more likely to get positive outcomes, and we give off positivity. Don't we all like win-win situations?

There is a catch to gratitude, and that catch is that you must grow to mean it. By this, I mean that first we say our expression of gratitude out loud, and as we do this, we try to feel it within. As the words leave your lips, allow the emotion to enter your body. The chances of you being alive in an infinite universe is a miracle in itself, but in case that still doesn't make you feel grateful, then we must train it. This is actually really simple to do. And like all things, it comes with practice. For some people who have grown up being ungrateful, negative or with feelings of entitlement, you will need even more practice. But like many of life's emotions, we can train them to serve us positively. First, you start by finding anything, no matter how small or large, to be grateful for, and then you express that gratitude to the universe.

"*I am grateful for* — insert thing you are grateful for — *thank you.*" As you do it, feel and believe that it is real. As neural pathways change in your head from the repetition, you will start to get better at it.

As you get better at showing gratitude and appreciation, you will see positive results start to flood into your life. Not only will you be saying many thank you's out to the universe, but you will also find that these thank you's resonate inwards as well. You will start to be thankful for the strong person you are becoming. Remember, you do not need to understand the mechanics of how this works just yet, you only need to know that it does work, and that it is extremely powerful. And on a side note start spreading that gratitude not only to the Universe but to people you see daily. You will be surprised at what positive things come back your way.

From a motivational standpoint, the first thing you start your day with is this acknowledgement of gratitude by saying what you are grateful for, and then you just leave it out there and go about your day. It takes minimal time and is extremely easy to do. This acknowledgement may be as simple as a single ten-second sentence of *I am grateful for...* or you could spend ten to fifteen minutes writing something down or meditating on what you are grateful for. You could even message someone you know and tell them what you are grateful for or why you are grateful for having them in your life. This is entirely up to you; do what works for you.

If you are still critical as I once was, your task is to experiment with gratitude and all the other information you have learned in this book. Never take any information at face value, testing something is the only way to see if it works. Try it for thirty days to start off with. Give it time to become habitual and see just how much more enjoyable your life becomes.

Gratitude is a positive double-edged sword. One edge invites goodness from the universe, and the other edge places a positive spin on any situation that enters your life, whether positive or negative. Everything that happens to us we can view as good or bad, positive, or negative. Viewing something negatively that has already happened will set us up for a lifetime of pain. This isn't to say that we must not initially experience some of this pain, in fact, part of healing and growth requires it. Pain can be a huge motivator. But to continue to stay in that mindset of pain will hurt you mentally and physically. You deserve happiness, and you must fight for it. Once the lesson has been learned from the situation, it's time to move out of that negative mindset into gratitude. Gratitude will allow healing both mentally and physically.

When we stress, we release cortisol, a fight or flight chemical. Cortisol is not meant to stay in the body for a long time. By choosing to stay negative about something that has already happened we continue to release cortisol. This suppresses our immune system and can make us sick. If something has already happened and is now out of your control, it's time to move forward and start focusing on all the things you can be grateful for and that are within your control. Be thankful for waking up on a summer morning, for the birds singing in the trees and for the sun that warms your face. Be thankful for the air that you breathe and for the baker who bakes fresh bread in the early hours of the morning.

Some people will feel that they don't deserve to feel good or that there is nothing to be thankful for. This is a thought habit that they have taught themselves over time. Like any thought habit, this pattern can be removed but will require work. It doesn't serve them any positive purpose staying in that mental space. And remember, for any negative thought that you remove, you must replace it with a positive thought. The raging wolf technique is excellent for this. Instead of asking, "Why is life so unfair?" You could say, "life can be unfair at times, but I'm so grateful for just how strong it has made me. And I look forward to the future with this new strength."

To be motivated on a daily basis, you should first and foremost be grateful that you are even a part of this amazing journey called life. We are indeed blessed to be alive in such a time of abundance that how can we not wake up each day with energy and motivation to embrace the day! Seek the beauty in everything and the beauty in everything will seek you.

Step 4 — Start Each Day with Achievement

"How you start your day will dictate what you accomplish throughout the day. That small but deliberate first step will change your life."

A motivated day requires an investment. That investment is a small token of achievement we need to pay every morning.

The second thing we should start our day with, after gratitude, is a small achievement. If you were looking for the holy grail of having a motivated day, this is it.

Through different stages in my life, I have tried out different methods. I didn't understand until my late twenties that a normal day isn't consistent. What I mean by this is that the morning of a day has a different feel and energy to it than that of mid-day. And the middle of the day has a different energy and feel than the afternoon and evening do. On top of this, our mind and body behave differently throughout the course of the day. We generally have more focus in the morning. We feel more tired in the middle of the day and in the evening. We generally start winding down before rest. Now, this is slightly different for different people with some feeling more energetic in the evenings and so on. If the energy throughout the day changes, then shouldn't we also plan what tasks we should do based on the time of day and on how we work individually? Absolutely right we should!

Whether you are a morning person or not, from the time you decide to wake you should be focused in on achieving one or more small tasks. Your goal here is to start the day by accomplishing something no matter how small. Then from there, you do tasks which are subsequently more challenging, and by the end of the day, you would have achieved a whole lot more than if you woke up and went headfirst into the day trying to achieve the big things straight away. Why? Because this method is much more sustainable in the long term. All you need to do is start the day with a small achievement. It is easy and non-threatening. This could be as simple as making your bed in the morning or replying to an email. You could put a load of washing on or go for a ten-minute walk. These simple tasks are not about achieving great things, they are solely about building momentum to then achieve the big tasks for the day.

The Motivation Station

Each night when we sleep, our body and mind are given an opportunity to recover, repair and to reset. When we wake in the morning, it is normal to slowly get out of bed, stretch out and adjust to the day. This is how the body and the nervous system work. It's similar to when you start your computer. It goes through a booting up process. Our body and mind have to boot up before we can hit it with the heavy tasks.

It would be great to be able to jump out of bed in the morning, hyper-motivated and ready to accomplish goals. Unfortunately, this isn't how motivation, the body or mind works nor is it sustainable. A motivated life requires doing things that are sustainable daily. If it isn't sustainable, then it is nothing more than an impulse. It won't last. I made this mistake for many years. I thought that I could try and get the big things out of the way first thing in the morning. This was great in theory, but I found that I couldn't sustain this for any amount of time, nor was it motivating for me while I was waking up. I created excuses and relapsed into failed mornings and thus failed days.

A common reason why people feel unmotivated or stuck is that the tasks that they seek to accomplish are too large, yet they want to accomplish those tasks straight away. They then get bogged down and end up doing nothing but loathing the task even more. Many texts talk about doing the hardest things first. On a day-to-day macro level, I don't believe that this is sustainable. If the first thing you do when you wake up is think, *darn, I have to complete "insert big task"*, then you aren't starting your day right or building the momentum and enthusiasm to attack the important tasks. Note that in saying this I also don't advocate *putting off* the essential tasks as this becomes a form of procrastination. Instead, we build up into this task by starting the day right. The way in which your day starts will dictate how much you have accomplished by the time your day ends. You are a well-tuned race car, warm up your engine and your tires before moving into the starting line to race. Start small and build up.

My day after gratitude starts with me making my bed (accomplishment) followed by a single set of ten bodyweight squats. I then put a load of washing on and write out my daily goals. This whole process can be done within five to ten minutes. After that time, I would have a clean looking bed (visual accomplishment) and have taken my body through a full leg range of motion (kinesthetic accomplishment) and have my goals for the day written out all while my clothes are being washed. These things may seem trivial, but they have a profound effect on my motivation for the day. By accomplishing something early, I put myself straight into an accomplishment mindset. This then builds momentum, and I am surprised with just how much I can achieve within that day.

What small habits or tasks could you start your day with? The way to measure if they are small enough is, are you able to do them on a consistent basis for a week or a month with minimal perceived effort? If not, then they are too big a task. Start small, I cannot stress this enough. If you haven't completed a task that should have been completed a long while ago, you haven't broken the task into small, sustainable enough pieces.

The success you have in the morning will dictate the success you have in your day. Wake up and start the day with achievement.

Step 5 — Deep Self-reflection

"By first looking inward, we are better able to travel outward."

One of the greatest attributes a person can have is the ability to be self-reflective in order to grow. To have something negative or positive happen and then to look inward in an attempt to understand themselves better show signs of a growth-oriented person. They do this to get a clear, unbiased understanding of all their thoughts and feelings associated with such an event.

People spend large amounts of time with the thoughts that run through their head. The problem is that there isn't a plan or an outcome that they set to deal with these thoughts. The thoughts show up at random, and we waste precious time thinking about them without a plan of what we want out of them. Imagination, creative thinking, and positive thoughts are the only ones we should allow to run away with our time. Self-criticism and tough lessons should have a purpose and an end-time to the thought. If we sit with negative self-criticism for too long, we are, in a way, feeding it and allowing it to stay.

What is the thought's purpose? If you did something wrong or something that hurt you or another person, then you need to experience the thought, and an element of the pain, to grow. But find what that lesson is and do it quickly. We are already way too good at hurting ourselves and inflicting our own form of karma for something we did wrong. Don't stay in that space. Somewhere in there is a lesson. The lesson is the good part that you need to extract from the experience so that you don't repeat something that hurts you or others.

What are the thoughts that constantly run through your head? What are the words you tell yourself when you need to do a task? We are taught to look outward for answers when the truth is, all the answers we seek already lay within us, but only if we are brave enough to travel inwards to find them.

Motivation is nothing more than a strong congruency between thought and action. If you are consistently doing what it is that you want to be doing with little to no internal conflict, then you are, by definition, motivated towards that task. If something is effortless for you to accomplish, then you are in a free-flowing state with it.

As a child, I would go with Father to our eight-acre farm. We grew sweet potato crops with papaya trees dotted throughout. Each weekend, we would bring a shovel and remove the weeds. At that time, weed killing chemicals were beyond our budget, and I'm glad they were. As a child, I didn't understand what we were doing. I said, "Why can't they live together?" Father replied that the weeds will continue to steal the nutrients from the crops so long as they share space. And so if we wanted a clear head, we also needed to weed out the negative thoughts.

Internal conflict and demotivating thoughts must be uprooted at the source. We have become very good at dealing with the symptom and not the root cause. This is like trying to remove a weed by chopping off one of its leaves, it will just grow back. We need to go deep into the earth and get our hands dirty to uproot it at the source. People don't like to get their hands dirty, but it's the only way to remove a negative thought for good.

In order for fruit and vegetables to grow, we should consistently weed this garden. The mind is no different. For clean, strong thoughts leading to clean strong action we must remove and weed out anything within our mind that would inhibit our productive thinking, and we must do it whenever we notice weeds or negative thoughts trying to enter our mind. If we allow them to grow, they spread and become much harder to remove.

Removing a negative thought isn't easy for most people. Chances are they have been saying it to themselves for a very long time reinforcing its hold within the mind. The longer they have had the thought, the harder it is to remove. Remember the saying: "You can't teach an old dog new tricks?" This is why. Old habits are hard to break. But they certainly can be broken.

Before we can remove a thought, we must acknowledge its existence. We do this by being self-reflective. Want to know what thoughts are holding you back? Spend the next week monitoring every thought that goes through your mind. Pay close attention to the thoughts a round times when you feel bad or demotivated. What happened in the lead up to you feeling negative? How did you react or feel when that trigger happened? How long did it take you to get back to a normal or more motivated headspace? What did you do to get there? Write this all down for a week, and you will start to see patterns of how your mind currently works. You will be shocked at the results. A good understanding of your problems is the first way to formulating a solution for them.

If we take an extreme example and look at a phobia such as the fear of dogs, we can better understand the principle of looking inward to solve our issues and build motivating thoughts. For someone who is fearful of dogs, they could have severe anxiety doing anything that puts them around a dog. Imagine your whole day being dictated not by your motivation to do something but by your fear and avoidance of something else. When we understand why we do, think, or feel things, we will have the ability to better liberate ourselves from the shackles of those things. We find that the majority of people with a dog phobia had, or viewed, a negative experience to do with dogs whilst in their childhood years. If the problem you have manifests as a fear, then nine times out of ten that fear originated somewhere in your past and programmed your subconscious mind to hold onto that fear to protect yourself. Rationalizing away such a fear will have little impact over removing it from our mind. First, we must understand where it came from, and then we must go through it as opposed to going around it. For someone fearing dogs, they will, at some point through their therapy, have to have a positive experience with a dog. They must go through their fear, not around it.

Before we are motivated and able to do the tasks we want to accomplish, we will have to bring the internal dialogue into the forefront and understand the reasons why we don't currently do them. What are the things that you consistently say to yourself when faced with a task that you want to do but don't end up doing? The more you know about how your mind thinks, the easier it will be to come up with solutions that change these thought patterns. This step is about understanding self and drawing a map of how you currently think before finding ways to banish those negative thoughts. Once you understand how your mind works, you can use a technique such as the raging wolf technique to replace negative thoughts.

Another extremely powerful tool is self-affirmations. An affirmation is when you talk to yourself in a targeted and positive way. I use affirmations daily to counteract any negative thoughts that may be trying to take root in my mind. Create your affirmations to suit your needs, goals and wants. You may say something like, "I am strong. I am smart, and I attract endless opportunities into my life." You then repeat this to yourself or others several times throughout the day. I think of an affirmation as a weightlifting session. I may say the phrase ten times and do four sets of this. I can do it daily or sometimes twice a day.

Once your internal self-talk becomes strongly positive, you'll find that you can do the affirmations less often. If you see that you start doubting or thinking negatively, then you need to do them more often. Affirmations, like exercise, require you to continue to express them throughout your life. Just like building muscle, you need to maintain them. Use it or lose it.

Don't fear becoming deeply self-reflective. Be open to self-honesty but make sure it is wrapped in self-love. Your goal is not to self-punish but to grow and to learn.

Pita Taufatofua

Step 6 — Remove Distractions

"When there is no distraction, there is clarity. With clarity comes the freedom to achieve great things."

A distraction is like a little thief that takes what isn't his. In the case of motivation, these things are time and focus.

I was a master procrastinator and would continuously look for distraction or reasons why I shouldn't do something. When it came to exercise and training this wasn't the case. But when it came to anything requiring administration skills or study, I failed miserably. My whole university degree was a battle between getting it done and doing anything except sitting and writing assignments. I would look for distractions everywhere. It was more enjoyable for me to use a broom and hose to scrub the side of the house where I was staying, to get it spotless, than it was to sit in front of my laptop and work. I would finish that and realize the garage needed cleaning, and so I would get that done next. After which, my newly bought bicycle chain would need to be re-oiled, and so forth. I could justify away not doing my assignments because in my head I was still accomplishing something. This was destroying my productivity.

How was it that I could be extremely motivated, never missing a training session in one area and extremely unmotivated, searching for distractions in another area? For starters, I liked training and hated university. Or more so, I hated doing an assignment or studying an area that I didn't believe was important or aligned with my life, despite choosing to undertake the degree. We all have strengths and weaknesses. The problem comes when we need to accomplish some of the things we don't want to do, so we get those we do want. I had to find a way to get through university as efficiently as possible. I had to starve my distractions. I recognized that I was a visual person, and if I saw anything while studying, I would find excuses to do things other than study. So what I did was blacken out my curtains, turned off all the lights, and only had a narrow beam from a table lamp to highlight my work. I literally couldn't see anything else other than my papers. I spent the majority of my university time, not in a library but in a dark room, reading. It didn't bring me joy, but it did bring me a degree and a better understanding of self.

Have you ever gone to do a task and got distracted? You started off thinking you were in a motivated state of mind and ended up not completing or even starting the task? Everyone has many specific distractions that are like kryptonite to them. These distractions can be general or task specific. Let's focus in on one of the biggest distractions, the mobile phone. We will use it as an example of the perfect distraction.

For the first time in human history, we have a device with seemingly unlimited access to information and programmed distractions, i.e. video games/apps, etc. And what makes it worse is that we carry our distraction device wherever we go and through whatever task we do.

Whilst the mobile phone has extreme productivity value, it also has extreme unproductivity potential. When they first came out, we, as owners, could be the masters of our phones. This mastery was largely possible because we couldn't do much but text and call on our phone. There was no social media, apps, or even color screens. As time and technology has progressed, our phone has become a master of us. It tells us what to do as we are trained to constantly monitor for that little beep or vibration that pulls us out of our motivation zone. How difficult it is for the human mind to focus on a task whilst also monitor for the notifications and ringtones pulling us into a separate task.

The mobile like most devices has strong work potential. If your work or task involves using a mobile to get a job done, then it is beneficial. But more often than not, it is nothing but a tool we use to distract ourselves from a task at hand. Just like the famous psychologist Pavlov, whose dogs were trained to respond to random ringing of a bell, we have been trained to do the same. The ring tone gives us small hits of dopamine. Dopamine, as you know, is the happy chemical we release as a reward for something. Alcoholics get a dopamine hit when they drink, drug addicts get a dopamine hit when they use drugs. But isn't dopamine a happy chemical? It sure is but in small doses or for true accomplishment reward. Having sporadic or random dopamine hit twenty-four hours a day has retrained our brain to be monitoring for it constantly. If one part of our brain is on alert for a stimulus, then it becomes unnecessarily difficult to focus on a single task.

The problem with always being in a dopamine hungry state is that it trains our brain to value short term small reward – distraction — over long-term large rewards — goals and purpose. We have become so dopamine-dependent that our attention span has dropped significantly over the past years. Just like a drug user, our dopamine levels have down regulated to the point that we need more just to get a bigger hit. And so the cycle continues.

The problem isn't that we attend to a task or that we have something to minimize our boredom, it is that we allow it to influence us during an important task. At these times, tools such as a mobile become a distraction. The cure for this is to start retraining our mind to take our focus back. We do this firstly by turning off ringtones and notifications during task time. We then minimize all notifications to essential calls or messages. Having notifications every time a social media message or email comes through isn't healthy to real-world living. Every time we enter the phone, we distract ourselves from the real world and become reliant on the digital world. This isn't bad at certain times, but as an all-day thing, it is most definitely harming your brain, mental health, and results.

Many different distractions pull us away from tasks. Each person has different distractions that affect them more than others. We focused on the mobile as it is universal and highlights many important points.

Let's look at the way people study. For some people, a café with a pair of headphones and their favorite music provides the best productivity. For others, a dark room or library with nothing but a small spotlight on their papers works best. Why is it that these two completely different environments both provide maximal productivity to different people? The answer is in the fact that all people are different and have different needs. The café person may be more productive knowing they are out and about amongst the hustle and bustle of a day. This amount of stimulation may wreak havoc on the quiet, dark room person. The key here is to recognize what works for you and what doesn't. We then use this information to devise a plan of attack for a specific task.

Setting up our environment to be conducive to motivation and productivity is our first step. If we start in the home what we see is the exact same set-up of many houses throughout the world. We have a lounge room with a television. We have a bedroom, more often than not, also with a TV, or many bedrooms or a study with their own set-up. Have you ever consciously stopped and thought about how your home is set-up? I'm sure if you walked through each room, you would find several things that would easily distract you from a task. Yet we still decide to do certain tasks in spaces which are distracting, and without even knowing that we are doing them.

There is a great saying that we should *starve our distractions, and yet feed our focus*. A method to do this is as follows:

Step 1 — Recognize what specific distractions stop you from one particular task. There is great power in knowing something that influences your actions. For each person, this will be different. Often, these distractions will be the same every time someone attempts a task. It could be having a mobile phone next to you whilst working on your laptop is distracting. It could be that studying at home leads to family distractions. Whatever they are, first recognize their existence.

Step 2 — Remove those distractions from your work area. This may mean that you have to remove yourself from those distractions, especially if those distractions are at home or with family. Remember that anything that steals your focus from your task is a distraction.

If you find yourself playing computer games when you should be working, then remove them. Easier said than done. But there are ways. Assigning time slots for both tasks *and* distractions is one of these ways. I could say that I will work for one hour straight, which allows me to be rewarded, and play for thirty minutes. There is no hard and fast rule. Each person is different. Some texts may say for each hour of work, assign yourself a five-minute break. While good in theory, this ratio of work to play is demotivating for a lot of people including myself. Through trial and error, I found that for every two hours of hard computer-based work, I needed the rest of the day off from computer tasks. While this may seem like an unproductive ratio, it works for me and my set of circumstances. What works for you? Remember the only rule for finding this ratio is that you must be able to do it consistently and that it must work for you.

Step 3 — The final step after removing distractions is to feed your focus. Each task has things that help feed its completion. If getting to the gym is the task, then that thing may be purchasing a new pair of shoes. If that task is computer-based, then an investment in a computer that motivates you to use it could be significant. Anything that makes the task easier or more motivating should be fed.

Once you start to recognize what specific distractions affect you negatively, your life will become much more productive. Remember that these distractions may provide short term joy, but that will be at the expense of your long-term happiness. Be ruthless in removing negative distractions, your future relies on it.

Step 7 — Streamline and De-clutter Your Life

"Streamline everything you do, and everything will become easier to do."

An unfortunate result of growing up in a one-bedroom house with so many people was that I was conditioned to be comfortable with clutter. It wasn't that my parents wanted a house full of stuff, but it was that it was inevitable that it would happen. Many people and a small space meant stuff was everywhere, and we were okay with it.

After being sent to boarding school, I found that I became a hoarder of stuff. There were two reasons for this: number one was that I grew up being comfortable in clutter; secondly, we were so poor in Tonga that I would see value in stuff that didn't really have value. Growing up on a farm made us resourceful, and so I would try to fix everything that was broken. I was now adding broken things into the clutter. I enjoyed a clean space, but I was very comfortable in the mess. This had a strong negative effect on my mindset. It wasn't inspiring, being in a place of mess, and it provided way too many distractions and unfinished projects. My mind became as unfocused as my living space.

If you look around at your living space what do you see? Is it neat and tidy or is there stuff everywhere? Your mind is your living space. If you want your mind to be free-flowing and uncluttered, then start with your environment. Everything you own exists in the real world but also takes up a piece of your mental real estate. Why? Because you know and think about everything you have. The more you have to think about the more distracted you become.

Our brain space is limited and so is our living space. If you prefer having more possessions, then increasing the size of your living space will help keep everything clutter-free. Buying a bigger house is one way to declutter, if that isn't currently an option, then the other is to remove stuff that has no special value to you. I suggest doing both.

It took me two years to declutter my life. Letting go of things which I had purchased or thought I could fix was very challenging. But I put in the work, and now my living space is as clear and free flowing as my mind. I am a reformed hoarder of stuff. My productivity grew massively, and my general feeling of peace also grew not having to worry about so many things.

Streamlining your life requires you to look at all aspects of your life and to see where you can make them flow more efficiently. In a business sense, a lot of time is put into streamlining processes, but we rarely do it in our personal life. Decluttering is one way to streamline your living space, and there are so many ways in which we can do this.

Master procrastinators look for reasons to not do a task, streamlining involves removing as many of those reasons as possible to make doing the task simple and without thought. If I told you that not having a clean pair of socks could prevent me from going to the gym, you probably wouldn't believe me. How could an Olympian be stopped from training by not having socks? Let me tell you, it had happened and happened in my early days when my focus was torn between multiple things such as university and training. On top of that, throw not having a gym towel or my house being so messy that I couldn't find my gym pass, etc.

And suddenly, my workout for the day was stopped in its tracks. I would justify staying home and doing something else other than training. I had to streamline my processes so that none of these things would happen and prevent my exercise sessions. The aha moment came when I recognized what was going on and how often it was happening. For the last twelve years, I haven't missed a training session simply because I always had a clean pair of socks and decided to keep my gym pass in the car. Simple right? The majority of your excuses have simple solutions.

The challenge isn't necessarily the streamlining process, it's recognizing precisely what distractions are affecting you, and what excuses you are using that prevent you from doing what you need to do. These things are repetitive and probably happen every time you go to do something. Stop for a second and think about what could be hindering your progress. What aspects of your life could be improved by streamlining and decluttering that area? When you look at my sock example, it probably seems extremely trivial. An ice-cold winter's evening with falling snow couldn't stop me from training; but a pair of socks could? If you want a motivated life, then you need to look at the small trivial things that hold you back as much as you need to look at the big things. This is the reality of distractions and excuses, it's often nothing more than a group of small things that add up.

What is your struggle? What needs to be streamlined? How can you make doing a task so simple that its execution just happens?

Write down the tasks you want to do consistently and write down the excuses and reasons you don't do them.

Now get clinical in finding ways to streamline those tasks.

If eating healthy is the challenge, then streamline this process by purchasing healthy food once a week on a day or time when you are consistently motivated. If that's too hard, have healthy meals sent to you once a week. If your challenge is exercise, then purchase motivating clothes and have them set out and ready the night before. If you have work that needs doing, then clean your desk and have your computer open and ready on the work at a time before it needs to be done. Make the task simple to start, and you will finish it with ease.

Be focused when it comes to cleaning your space and streamlining your processes. Look at your living environment and think of it as being your mind. Is it messy and unmotivating or is it free-flowing and uncluttered? Now get to work!

Step 8 — Make the Task Smaller

"The only way to move mountains is to start with small stones."

This step changed my life. Being a master of motivation, I always wanted to do big things. I wanted to accomplish things that no one else could achieve, and I wanted to do them right away. But it never went to plan. I had read that we should attack the big goals head on, and so I did. I would throw everything I had at a target and most of the time would fail or would only be motivated for a short amount of time. It was exhausting and unmotivating, attacking a big goal head on every day for years. I eventually found out that sustainable progress towards those goals came not by attacking the big target but by breaking down those goals into tasks I could sustainably attack.

One of the biggest reasons we procrastinate or feel overwhelmed is because a task is much too big. It becomes so overwhelming to do such a task that we end up doing everything except that task. The following point is critical to getting something done. However big the task, break it down into its smallest possible sub-tasks. By breaking something down, we remove the overwhelming feeling of just how big the scope is and focus in on the manageable microtask. If you wanted to move a mountain, you must do it stone by stone. To carry a whole mountain away would be extremely difficult. To carry a small stone away over and over again would be much more achievable, sustainable and thus motivating. If we were to work smart instead of just hard, then we would bring in machinery like trucks that can carry more stones. We start slowly by making a plan, organizing machinery, and then slowly starting to move stones, as we progress on the mountain moving journey.

Let's revisit our New Year's resolution. On the first day of January, we created and then attacked our goals for the year with gusto. A few weeks later, we are right back where we started. One of the biggest mistakes I see with people trying to become motivated is that they start too big too early. They are excited to attack their goal for whatever reason, but their habits and self-discipline aren't on the same level as their excitement. They soon get demotivated and fail, thus strengthening their inner dialogue that they can't achieve their goals.

So how small should we break the task down to? This is person specific. Let's take an example of someone wanting to go to the gym consistently to achieve their desired body. For an athlete, a small, broken-down task may be to do three training sessions a week. For someone who hasn't trained in years, the smallest possible task may just be to think about training for a week. I'm sure that sounds extremely easy for the vast majority of people but for certain people that may be all they can manage in their current condition. As they were able to achieve a small task, they then build momentum and strength to accomplish bigger tasks. Start small and build up.

We are too hard on ourselves. It seems that we only want to reward ourselves when we reach the big goal. But no big goal gets achieved without achieving small sub-goals. The most important thing is progressing forward however small that progress is. It would be great to be able to tackle the whole task at once and just get it done. But "just getting it done" doesn't always work because we become overwhelmed and soon stop. And so we fail, end up hating the fact that we failed, and we find ourselves in the space of self-loathing. We then give up on the goal because we hate the feeling of failing and want to avoid that pain in the future.

I want you to think of a task that you've been struggling to accomplish. Now I want you to break that task into its smallest possible parts. Most people when they do this don't break the task small enough. I want you to break it down so small that it is impossible for you not to be able to achieve the smallest possible sub-task. As mentioned earlier, that may be simply 'thinking about the task' once a day. Yes, that is how small I want you to go. Now you may be saying that thinking about the task won't get it done. If you haven't done it, then you're already not getting it done. Stop thinking about achieving the task and start thinking about being consistently able to do something, however small, towards its accomplishment. As you build habits and self-discipline, you can increase the size of the task that you can do consistently. If for whatever reason you find you reach a task that you stop working on steadily, then you need to stop and go back a step to a smaller sized task.

Still to this day, I break down tasks to be so small that people would laugh if they knew how small I broke them down to. I want you to get a firm grip on this so I will give you some examples from my own life. If I need to mow the lawn, then I may dedicate a whole day to just pulling the lawn mower out and having it ready (a task that takes three minutes). Next, I may dedicate an entire day to getting fuel from the fuel station (a task that takes ten minutes). I may then dedicate another day to clearing the yard of objects that may impede my mowing flow (a task that takes five minutes). And on day four, I mow with nothing to hamper my task. This is an extreme example. I'll often do all the tasks on one day, but if I feel any resistance to mowing the lawn, I will break down the task as such.

The whole day isn't sacrificed for those sub-tasks. The mowing part of my day is. I may spend five minutes clearing objects from my yard, and then go about my day, as usual, not thinking about mowing the lawn. Mowing and gardening is therapeutic to me. It helps me reconnect with nature, and so the actual task is enjoyable.

If my big goal was to do seven days a week of Taekwondo training, then I could probably do it in the first week, but I don't. I know it won't be sustainable until I've built the habits to sustain it by consistently repeating the task. Instead, I would plan to build up to that level of training over a two-month period. The first week I might do one training session. The second week, I may do two training sessions, and so forth, until I can maintain that level of training indefinitely. Our New Year's resolution goals of training every day fail because people go straight from zero to hero and haven't built the hero habits and qualities.

Any step forward is progress, and progress is motivating. If you have been struggling to achieve a goal, you are most probably overwhelmed by the size of the task. Break down your goals to sustainable chunks, and your life will change for the better.

Pita Taufatofua

Fear and Nerves

"Overcoming fear requires strength. We all have the strength needed to be fearless."

To accomplish great things, we must be fearless. We must stand tall in the face of adversity and deliver the best of us. To do this, we need to prepare our mind for the challenges that will come, long before they arrive. Fear is a response that every one of us has to perceived danger. Being nervous is fearing an uncertain outcome. Or said another way, not knowing what will happen makes us nervous. As a living being, we developed fear and nerves in order to keep us safe from things like dangerous animals or warring tribes. But what has happened with the evolution of a relatively safe society is that we still have a strong fear response without having nearly as much actually to fear.

A person going to present a paper in front of a room full of peers may have the same fear response as one of our ancestors preparing for war. A room full of judgmental peers won't have nearly the same danger level as a life-threatening situation. It is a disproportionate response. Yet public speaking is one of the highest rated fears that people have in modern society. In our mind, we cannot always differentiate this irrational fear from rational fear. We may know that it is irrational, but we still have that fear response anyway.

The level of fear you feel whether rational or irrational is real to you. I can't tell you that what you feel before attempting something that scares you isn't real. The reason being is that you still get that fear response which affects you emotionally, mentally, and physically. What I can say is that like every other lesson in this book with the proper training you can overcome or largely minimize the irrational fears that you have. You will do this by recognizing and articulating your fears, and then preparing a course of action to take, long before you feel them so as to dull their influence over you.

It is incorrect to tell you that all of your fears will be removed. Some of them serve a very real and beneficial purpose. Avoiding danger because you fear a dangerous situation will keep you alive. These aren't the fears you want to control. Entering a war zone, dangerous area or walking on a steep ledge when there is no need to, isn't fearlessness but senselessness. No one of right mind should risk life and limb just to prove their level of fearlessness.

People ask me why I rarely if ever get nervous. Even standing at the start line of an Olympic skiing race at the Winter Olympics did not trigger that fear response. The truth isn't that I never get nervous or fearful but that I never allow it to control me. I have learned to become the master of my emotions and not the other way around, and so will you. I got this way from training. Albeit I didn't purposefully embark on this fearlessness training, but it was coincidental from years of competing and fighting in Taekwondo and martial arts tournaments. There is very little more fear-provoking than when you prepare to fight someone in full contact combat as has been the case many a time in my career. The days leading into the tournament your level of anxiety, nerves and fear slowly increase. Will I win, or will I get knocked out in front of everyone watching? Will I leave the tournament with injuries or worse? How will people look at me if I get kicked in the face or cower from a well-timed blow? Will my career be over if I can't beat a fighter who I should easily beat? What will people say about my performance? So many questions would run through my mind before every single tournament. Two heavyweight fighters with the very real ability to hurt the other is a rational fear. There is the possibility of pain or death. Years of going through this process taught me that most other things I would encounter in life would never come close to the level of fear that I, and every other fighter, would have before a match. I am not advocating taking up contact sports to train your fear response, but it certainly can help.

What I will show you is how I used that fear to go through a mental process so that even though you feel it, you will never let it control you. Contrary to what you may see on T.V, there isn't a professional fighter who doesn't feel some level of fear or nervousness before a match. They are just better at controlling that fear response.

Below are three steps I would use to approach the fear before a fight. These three steps can be used in any situation whereby you feel fear or anxiety about doing something. Because of the nature of life, there will always be situations which are out of your control and may happen regardless of what we do. We can't control everything that may cause us to fear, but we can plan in advance for how we respond to these situations should they arise.

Step 1 — Gather knowledge of your personal fear response

Like clockwork and before every match, I would feel the exact same emotions at roughly the same times. I would know who I was fighting before fight day. The match schedule would be released days or weeks before the tournament. This was a double-edged sword. On one hand, we could prepare for a specific fighter, but on the other, we could leave ourselves open for days or weeks of worry about fighting a particular opponent. If the fighter were a highly skilled and dangerous opponent, I would have a fear response. This was normal; my mind saw the danger and wanted me to avoid it to stay safe. The problem was that the threat was in the way of my goals and I would, therefore, need to go through it. In my early career, I would make the mistake of playing in my head the scenarios where the opponent could beat or hurt me. I would be so caught up in what he could do, and I would lose sight of just how good I was or what I could do. Have you ever been in a situation where you were so focused competitively on someone else's ability that you forget about how great your own level of knowledge or skill was?

In this step, your goal is to gather information on how you personally react when faced with a situation that causes you fear or anxiety. The more you go through these situations, the more information you can gather on how you naturally respond to fearful situations. Once you know how you naturally respond, then you can look at correcting and improving this. You can turn fear into excitement. Write down what your personal fear response is to something that you are scared of. What goes through your mind when you approach a fearful situation? Is it rational or irrational fear? Does it happen hours, days, or weeks before the situation or is it always there? Try to get all the information you can about how your mind deals with fear.

Step 2 — Understand your excuses

Your next task is to list the excuses you come up with leading into a stressful situation. What is it that you tell yourself to get out of the situation? Or what is it that you tell others to try and pre-minimize the effect of having a negative outcome from the situation?

Before I had trained my fearless muscle, I would have a list of excuses. Some I would tell myself and some I would tell others. Firstly, I would look for excuses for why I shouldn't fight. In my mind I would justify things like, I don't need to fight, I could pull out and focus on a later tournament, the opponent was too good for me to beat, there were too many people watching, and I don't want to disappoint them, therefore, I can feign an injury etc. To say these petty excuses didn't go through my head almost every match would be a lie. They did, and sometimes they still do. In this step, you must be honest with yourself, and you must understand from a non-judgmental viewpoint what goes through your head when you are scared or nervous. You can't correct something that you can't understand. Write down your excuse list. Be honest with yourself when you do this. Some of these excuses you will use often and in many different areas where you feel fear. If you notice you consistently blame someone else for something, then now is the time to write that excuse down. If we want to develop ourselves, this is the perfect time to be honest with who we are, and how we function.

There is no weakness in having fearful thoughts. The issue comes when you don't act upon them in a way that minimizes their effect on you. If you make the same mistakes over and over, then you are robbing yourself of growth. Years of finding excuses taught me that it wasn't bad that they would enter my mind, but that it was only bad if I would act upon them and allow them to influence me negatively. Not once in my whole martial arts career did I pull out of a fight. I lost many times, but I always stepped into the ring against whoever stood in front of me. I never once pulled out of a fight despite the fear and excuses in my head. By understanding my excuses, I knew that it was normal for them to come, but I would never act upon them and allow them to prevent me from competing.

Just because excuses find their way into your thoughts, does not mean that you should entertain them. The more times you go through a challenging process, the more times you will be training and thus strengthening your fearlessness muscle.

Step 3 — Have a plan

Fear and nerves cloud our judgement and ability to make the best decisions for us. When fear takes over, its primary purpose is *fight, flight, or freeze*. Fear heightens our senses, and this can either give us butterflies in our stomach or ensure that our nervous system is firing at an optimal and beneficial level. Getting butterflies, sweating, and having a panic attack right before giving a presentation to your companies' board of directors, isn't going to help your presentation. Your fear response in this case only serves a harmful purpose. What you need to do is have a pre-made plan for what to do in case this fear and anxiety response happens.

I knew before each fight that I would feel fear and find excuses. I knew that that fear would be worse the day before the fight. I also knew that the excuses would start close to a week before the fight and end the morning of the fight. I had been in that position so many times that I knew exactly what would happen and when. So I made a plan. Whenever an excuse for why I shouldn't fight came into my head, I would start telling myself all the reasons why I should fight. This was a form of the raging wolf technique. The night before a match I would have all my match gear ready so that when I woke up on match day morning, everything was ready to go, and there were no barriers to me showing up. Adding the stress of looking for the right uniform and gear on match morning would only add to the anxiety of match day, and so I pre-planned to remove that stress the night before. I had my song and music playlist ready. I had chosen songs that would give me a feeling of happiness and power. Music has the ability to do this.

My coach, Master Paul, who also would compete as a fighter, did things differently from me. Before a match, he would go into a bubble and talk to nobody, giving him his best performance. On the other hand, and after trying this out, I found that it didn't work for me and my personality. I saw that my best performance came by going into my bubble on the way to the tournament but then opening right up and being chatty with everyone I could on the day of competition. The feeling of happiness always gave me my best performance. And this was my plan. I created my plan for game day long before game day came. By the time it was time to fight my competitors, I was in my best frame of mind. The goal was always to show up and always to give my absolute best. Winning was a by-product of giving my best. Sometimes the competitor would also show up with their best, and sometimes on that day, their best was better than mine. I always finished the match happy that I had left the best version of me on the mats. There is peace in knowing you gave your best version of yourself regardless of the outcome.

Create your plan long before you reach a situation that you fear. Plan for contingencies and Murphy's law. Murphy's law states that some things may and will go wrong. Plan for what you can, but also plan for something coming up that is out of your control, then you will go with the flow and leave your best on the mats, so to speak. Know in advance that you will experience the fear or nerves, and that is normal. Practice for the fearful situation at full intensity and create your plan around this feeling. In Taekwondo we have a saying, "Train hard; fight easy." Prep well, and the actual fear-provoking event will be easy. Most importantly, always show up.

What is it that you fear? For some people there is fear of failure, and for others, there is a subconscious fear of success. Two completely opposite fears. Yes, being successful can be scary, especially if your mind isn't aligned with being successful. This can cause you to sabotage your own success, or even relationships, because you don't feel worthy of them. But you are worthy, you deserve all the good things that will come into your life regardless of what others around you may have once told you. Listen to that voice inside that says you are enough and silence the one that says you aren't worthy.

If you fear failure which is also very common, then this can be used as a great motivator. You want to be careful though that you don't hyper-focus on avoiding failure, and then fail to see your own future success. Your fear of failing should drive you to want more. There are countless examples of highly motivated and successful people who came from very challenging backgrounds. Failing was not an option, and they used their challenges as fuel to propel them into a positive and successful life.

Are you scared of being judged by others? Truth is, what you think of yourself will have an infinitely greater positive impact on your life than what others actually think of you. You are the only person that will live with yourself twenty-four hours a day every day of every year. Other people are only guests in your life. Be kind to yourself. I have met many people who won't step foot into a gym or sports class for fear of what the people there will think of them. People are funny creatures. We always think others are judging us when in reality, those other people are, in fact, wondering if they are being judged, and mostly don't care about what we are doing, but we think they do. We project our thoughts on other people. This is a dilemma of human vanity, thinking everyone is here to judge us. Understand that everyone is just trying to get by the best they can in their own life.

When I lost against the world champion from Iran in my first match at the Olympic Games, it could have been an extremely humiliating experience, had I let it become one. Billions of people across the globe had seen me walk out shiny and strong, covered in coconut oil, at the Rio Olympic opening ceremony. They wanted me to win a medal and get that storybook finish, but it wasn't to be. The stadium was sold out to the point where I couldn't even get Father a ticket to my own match.

Years of fearlessness training had set me up well, and my nerves were in check; they were not going to get the better of me. Despite this, I was very slow to start the match, and by the end of the first round of my only fight, my opponent and his long flexible frame had managed to score unanswered head kick points on me before I even knew what was happening. A kick to the head region was worth three points in a Taekwondo match, and flexibility and height was the new name of the game. I had never fought a six-foot, six-inch world champion whose legs could reach my head from what seemed like miles away. It's tough to find a sparring partner of that stature so when I went up against him, I was in a situation I hadn't been in before. The score had run away from me before I had even gotten started. My coach was yelling at me to wake up, and I couldn't even hear him. The second round I did much better, and my focus had changed from defensive fighter to just throw everything at him and seeing what would happen. I couldn't make the Olympics and not score on this guy.

Just before the match ended, I managed to score against him. To me, at that point, it felt like a huge victory. What was even more amazing was that the whole stadium was up on their feet chanting: TONGA! TONGA! TONGA! I had lost the match by points but by controlling my nerves and being fearless in my final round to get that evasive point I had won the crowd. I shook my opponents' hand and left the Olympic ring with a big smile on my face. We think people only judge our performance, the truth is that people judge our character and also how hard we try. Regardless of what people would think of my performance I was happy and content that I had finally woken up and given my all despite not winning a medal. I left the stadium with a smile. People's judgements of us are overly magnified in our mind, it's our goal to focus not on what they think but on how we think about ourselves.

To overcome your fears, you must train in the situations that you will face long before you face them. This will have an effect of changing your irrational fear to excitement as your mind now recognizes that these situations aren't as scary as they appear. If your goal is to become an actor, then you will practice delivering lines with people watching you long before you walk into a casting office. If you fear public speaking, then you will talk to every person you come across in day to day life, whether it be the youth that bags your groceries at the grocery store or your colleagues at work. Force conversations as a means of practice.

If you fear failing, try the same thing in different ways. If you fail, then you are one step closer to succeeding. Laugh when you fail and ask yourself what lesson you received from that failure. I would often laugh and joke with my brothers and friends about my biggest failures. The huge ones became excellent jokes that would light up and provide laughter to any conversation. Stop being so hard on yourself and realize that not only will your failures put you closer to your successes, but they can be hilarious stories for the rest of your life.

If you fear judgement, then it's time for you to do something to take away people's power over you. You should have pre-thought-out responses to possible criticisms that people may use to attack you. Or you could work on developing your own self-validation by practicing ignoring non-constructive criticism. These days I feel sorry for people who constantly criticize others. I think that their life must be so painful that they feel the need to offset that pain by attacking others. Having sympathy and trying to understand people's intentions will help build your resilience and understanding about life.

Fear is one of our strongest motivators. Is your fear motivating you in the right or the wrong direction? If it is scaring you away from doing something positive, then you must deal with that fear. The only way to deal with fear is to go through it. It is impossible to run away from irrational fear; it will always catch you or be waiting for you in some other area of your life. Once you defeat that fear and anxiety, you put it to rest forever. Contrary to what people may have said about me lacking a t shirt, I did in fact have one when I was a young boy that read, *wherever the fear may be, look it in the eyes,* and that is what you should do. Stare that fear down like the warrior that you are!

Being strong isn't about lacking fear, but it is about controlling fear. The strongest people aren't entirely fearless; instead, they know when fear is real, and when it is a construct of our mind. They plan for how they will approach it, whether rational or irrational, should it be beneficial for their growth.

Whatever it is that you fear, you must overcome. Your emotions should be used to add flavor to your life and not to control your life. Practice the things that you fear, and you will find that your fears decrease in magnitude. Plan for stressful situations long before they happen so that logic helps you think through your emotions. You are the master of your destiny; you are the captain of your ship. Practice adjusting the sails long before the storm hits, and you will become fearless during the storms that may come. You will be like the mountain, unmoving in the face of gale-force winds. Instead of finding excuses, you will say to the fear, "Send me your best, and I will send you mine!"

Pita Taufatofua

When Everything is Going Wrong

"Before every mountain, there is a valley. Everything goes wrong just before it goes right."

Your times of greatest growth will come right after your times of deepest pain. Let me say it again. Your times of greatest growth will come right after your times of deepest pain. So long as you make the decision to keep moving forward, then growth follows pain. It is just the way life works. Now don't get this wrong and assume that we must have pain to grow. That is not the case. With deliberate and focused work, we can build resilience long before pain finds us. But the sometimes-uncertain nature of life means that there will be pain that is out of our control. It could be the loss of a loved one, the loss of a job or health problems.

I cannot begin to tell you just how many times I have seen growth following extreme pain not only with clients but in my own life. We even had a saying in the homeless shelter, for young people going through drug addiction. We said that they would probably need to hit rock bottom before they made one of life's most important choices. To stay there or to bounce back. For the heavily drug addicted clients, it sometimes felt as though we needed to wait for them to hit that point before we could do our work to help them. In those times, what we did do was let them know that whatever they were going through was all part of a journey. We would provide unconditional care and support no matter what lows they reached. This was our way of trying to cushion their fall, not so that they didn't feel the pain, but so that they knew there were people there for them even in their darkest moments. They had to experience some of the pain in order to grow.

My goal when a client hit their version of rock bottom was to level off the pain and let them see that it was never as bad as they thought it was. I would highlight to them that despite being at rock bottom, they were still able to function and even have moments of joy. Removing the fear around rock bottom gave them not only hope but the excitement that they could now work on climbing up to a new high, even higher than they had been before.

In all my years working I never once had a client who couldn't pull them self out of the depths. Yes, there were young people who still to this day have challenges with addiction, but all those who had made that choice to grow would grow. All they had to do was make a choice not to stay in the pits of pain, and then we could provide them with the tools to work themselves out of those times.

I have seen drug addiction take absolutely everything from someone and leave them with nothing. Heavy drugs altered a client's mental chemistry to the point that, not only were they fighting their own demons, but they were feeding these demons at the same time as trying to defeat them.

As a student of life and long before becoming an Olympian I would study people who were successful and people who were on their way to success. Something I noticed was that it didn't matter what level of financial wealth someone had, they were still exposed to similar challenges. I saw famous Olympians and athletes hit rock bottom not long after winning medals and achieving their dreams. I saw both athletes and celebrities take to all kinds of recreational and prescription drugs to numb the pain of what was going on deep inside them. I saw many great people self-sabotage to the extent that you would never think that they could have once been successful. Rock bottom affects everyone. The difference with celebrities was that their rock bottom was highly publicized. It is the catch-22 for being someone of influence. Their success gave them great opportunities, but their challenges gave them magnified and publicized pain. No one will be able to avoid life's challenges. The goal isn't to run from them but to train yourself to know that you are strong enough to handle whatever may come your way.

Be strong in your convictions and make the best decision as to how you decide to live your life. Don't be negatively swayed by peers no matter how close they are to you. True love is people being able to value and respect your decisions. Self-love is being able to value and respect your body, your mind and your future.

I found that if someone needed large doses of detrimental drugs just to feel happy, then there was an imbalance happening somewhere in their foundation. Their life purpose and search for happiness were often misaligned. The problem with a lot of those highs was that they weren't sustainable and would be followed by lows and an ever-spiraling movement towards rock bottom. Now you may be questioning why I said that people shouldn't fear rock bottom. It's not that they shouldn't fear it, it's that plunging yourself towards it with movements of self-sabotage is a recipe for disaster. Rock bottom should happen when there are problems out of your control or while you are working toward something positive, not because you're aiming for rock bottom. Remember, once you get there it could be a time for either massive self-growth or, if you keep with your ways, a time for prolonged self-suffering.

The thought of hitting rock bottom is terrifying for most people. I have hit it several times in my life. In my case, it wasn't because I was spiraling out of control, but because I was working so hard that I lost my center. Life is strange like that. On top of that, there were things that were out of my control that exacerbated the problems. However, you arrive at rock bottom doesn't affect your outcome so long as you make the conscious choice not to stay there.

I would like to share with you three of the times I hit my version of rock bottom as an adult. The first time was during the global financial crisis. I had two jobs and lost both of them on the very same day as both companies were failing, and all employees were being made redundant. I lost all access to an income. On top of this, I had just booked a ticket for myself and my partner to fly to Europe on a one-month holiday, all while returning to no job. I thought my plan B of having multiple jobs would keep me safe, life had other plans. Travelling to Europe was a dream of hers, and I was in the business of wanting people to achieve their dreams, and so I invested all I had to make the holiday special. Being a university student at the time this wasn't much, but it was all I had saved.

I remember on the last day of the European trip, sitting in the train in London's Paddington station and nervously asking my partner for fifty pence, so I could purchase my ticket on the train to get to the airport. How humiliating. There is nothing harder for me than to ask for money; this was a massive blow to my ego. The trip was ill-fated from the start and ended up in a whole lot of disagreement. Upon arriving back home, I experienced a back injury when cycling up a steep hill. Not only was I financially broke and my relationship on the rocks, but I couldn't even physically move to help myself bounce out of my rock bottom. My relationship failed, my body failed, and I had no job or ability to move and get across to interviews to get a new job. I lay there for two weeks, feeling every bit of the pain, patiently waiting for my back to heal so that I could do something about it. That was one of my first rock bottoms as a young adult. I had to use years of self-discipline and all my martial arts training to fight off the negative thoughts that were trying to enter my head.

Lucky for me I had some pretty good tools to help make that happen. I worked very hard to focus on nothing but the positive things that were in my life. Once I could move, I applied for several jobs and got offered positions in all the jobs I had applied for. I had been at rock bottom long enough; I had no interest in staying there. Even now as I write these words, I cringe at sharing the details of my rock bottom. Of being an adult and having to ask my partner for fifty pence so I could make a train to the airport. One of the greatest lessons I learned from rock bottom was that it was temporary so long as you worked hard not to stay there.

Have you ever experienced rock bottom? Have you ever had so many negative things happen to you all at once that it was just too overwhelming? Peoples version of rock bottom will vary in magnitude. There will be many of you who read my first rock bottom experience and see it like a walk in the park. This point is all relative to you and what you consider painful. It isn't a contest nor should you ever measure this point against others. It is nothing more than a cumulation of negative experiences that put you at a deep low point.

Before we reach our mountain, we must first go through our valley. There is no mountain without a valley. By the time I reached my next life low point, I was much better prepared. For months leading up to the Rio Olympic qualifiers, everything was going wrong. I was in the early stages of starting a relationship with someone special whom I had known for many years, but at the same time, I was trying to focus on training. The vigorous nature of Taekwondo training had meant that my knees were failing, and I was constantly pulling muscles in my hamstrings from all the kicking I was doing. My car would break down almost weekly, and I would have to have it towed over a hundred kilometers as my Taekwondo gym was in a different city to where I lived. My finances were again struggling as I had put every last dollar I had into training and rehabilitation costs. At this point, I had no sponsors and Tonga had no money to send me to the Oceania Olympic qualification tournament in Papua New Guinea. I had saved just enough for me but not for my coach. The day before the tournament, I got a call saying that someone in Tonga wanted to help buy our ticket, and so we flew to Papua New Guinea. There is a rule in Taekwondo where weigh-in is at a set time the day before the competition. One of the other Tongan athletes had missed weight, and we were stuck on the wrong side of the city sitting in a sauna hoping he would sweat those last kilograms of weight off. I was getting extremely nervous as the time for weigh-in was coming to an end, and we weren't even close to the weigh-in location. I asked the driver if we could leave and left our other athlete still in the sauna; he never made weight.

We arrived at the weigh-in area one minute before the closing time. The referees facilitating this assumed there were no more athletes and were starting to walk

away. I ran in and yelled for them to stop and to allow me to weigh in as there were still seconds left, literally seconds. They unenthusiastically told me about the rules but obliged. I weighed in and the next day won the tournament to become the first athlete from Tonga to compete in Taekwondo at the Olympics ever.
Everything went wrong just before it went right. I still laugh about the experience, but had I given in to any of those pressures, or had I stopped because of the challenges, then I would never have made it to the Olympics. The universe rewards perseverance through adversity.

The Motivation Station

If I am to explain the way it works, then the easiest way to think of it is what I call the Donkey Kong analogy from the hugely successful arcade game. In Donkey Kong, a character called Mario must fight his way up through different levels in order to defeat the giant ape, Donkey Kong, and rescue the Princess from his clutches. As you work your way through the levels of the game, you notice that everything gets harder and harder. Right up to the point that on the last level, Donkey Kong throws all his barrels and everything he has at you. If you keep going, then you will be able to defeat him and rescue the princess, i.e. get your reward. In life, we don't often know that we are on the last level before we get our reward. All we see is that everything is going wrong and life seems extremely unfair in those moments. And this is where most people quit. They quit just before they are about to level up, just before they are about to receive their reward. When you have been working hard towards a goal and find that everything is going wrong, then that isn't a time to quit; that is a time to get excited because you are on the verge of succeeding in what it is that you are destined to achieve.

The last time I hit rock bottom was again just before the Winter Olympics. People assume that because of my new-found stardom from the Summer Olympics that life would then be a walk in the park. Nothing could be further from the truth. I had announced my second sport, and so there was a lot of pressure on me to Qualify. The pressure I didn't mind, in fact, I enjoy high-pressure situations. And even failing doesn't faze me so long as I've given everything I've got. What was challenging was that a lot of the winter sports companies don't exactly like us "exotic" countries as we aren't podium winners, well not yet. And we didn't fit into their perceptions of what a winter athlete should look like. There is somewhat of a feeling of 'you aren't meant to be here', an elitism that I had never experienced in Taekwondo. I had made the assumption that because I was a well-known athlete that ski companies would jump at the opportunity to sponsor me and help me on my journey. This was not the case. A lot of the major ski companies thought it was some big joke because there was no way I was ever going to qualify for the Olympics in under one year of starting a new and extremely tough sport.

I remember writing to a large ski company asking what size skis they recommended I should use as I was told they had the best skis. Their reply was, "We recommend that you use another brand of skis as you aren't good enough to use ours." And so right up until I qualified. that was the feel coming out from some of the major ski companies. Their tune changed once I had qualified, but by that stage, I was happy with my new and only pair of skis (when other Olympians had close to forty choose from), and my ego remained intact.

Again, everything in the qualification was going wrong. We had run out of funds. I had lucrative acting and public speaking deals offered to me after Rio, but I turned them down to pursue cross country skiing and the chance at becoming a two-sport Olympian. I travelled with my two competitors, now friends, from Chile and Mexico to close to fifteen countries in eight weeks and struggled in many of the races with poor equipment and difficult conditions. I needed just one more good race to qualify after failing in close to ten races. On the last race of the last day of the qualification period, we flew on one-way tickets to Iceland. My brother had purchased my ticket on air travel points. We could only afford one-way tickets. Upon arriving we found that a snowstorm had shut down the airport in Ísafjörður, where the race was to be, and there was no flying there. Everything was going wrong. From my past experiences, this had me excited. And so for three days we drove through the snowstorm, unable to see the roads, in order to get to the last race. Donkey Kong was throwing everything he had at us including the kitchen sink and giant snowballs. The snowstorm had led to several avalanches that covered the roads. We planned to drive as far as we could to the first avalanche, leave the car on the side of the road and hike the remaining twenty-five kilometers to the race. We didn't know if the car would still be there once we got back, and we couldn't afford the insurance on it, but we took the risk. We were ready for bankruptcy, or a warm Iceland jail, if it meant we may qualify. We were going to leave no stone unturned in our quest to become Winter Olympians. Luckily for us, the avalanches had been cleared moments before we arrived — just as the snowstorm was ending. We were able to drive on through the last twenty-five kilometers to the little town of Ísafjörður.

We finally arrived late the night before the race. The conditions on the track were terrible. The snowstorm had made the racetrack overly soft; my one pair of skis were sinking into the snow making for a very tough track testing session. Things weren't looking good for myself and Madrazo for the race the next day. It was ten o'clock at night, and I saw the man grading the track in his big machine was carrying a few extra kilos around his belly on his large frame. I casually walked up to him and said that we *heavier guys* need to stick together. And if there was any way he could have the track up to world-class level by the next morning. He looked at me and said he would see what he could do. He must have

The Motivation Station

been there all night as the next morning the track was rock hard. The perfect conditions for my one pair of skis built for icy snow. With the performance of my life, I on the last race of the qualification period pulled out a time that allowed me to qualify for my second Olympics. We had gone through our valley before we reached our mountain. And we were rewarded. If you find that everything is going wrong despite all the hard and smart work you are doing, then that isn't a time to quit. That is your time to push even harder. Everything goes wrong just before it goes right so long as you keep powering forward. Don't stop, your reward is waiting on the other side of your pain!

Pita Taufatofua

Fail Happy and Forgive Yourself Quickly

"Be both your most honest critic and your most forgiving friend."

My greatest blessing growing up was that I had parents who showed unconditional love. This meant that when I succeeded, they loved me the same as when I failed. I can't begin to explain the profound effect that had on my fearlessness to try big things. I felt invincible. If I got gold, I received love, and if I came last, I also received love. Some would say that their style of parenting was too soft and that kids need a firmer hand. Make no mistake, I also had very strict parents, but they were tough in the areas of discipline, humility, sharing, looking after others, and work ethic. If my siblings or I were disrespectful to an adult or family member, my father would pull out his slipper to swat my hand. As discipline, it worked with me. He had no anger, only a desire to help me improve. I didn't want to do better at that age — I wanted to do what I wanted, without repercussions. Discipline set a clear boundary.

Each time I crossed the line, I would look back and realize I wanted to behave better. I was a very quick learner; rarely would I repeat the thing that I had done wrong. And never were we disciplined for a result in an area where we tried and failed. In fact, we were never disciplined for any result. If I got a bad grade in school, they would encourage me rather than punish me. There is a difference between discipline and love.

My parents, throughout their discipline, always showed love and caring. Instead of fearing them, I wanted to do well for them, and this made me try harder. They fostered an environment whereby learning and failing and trying again was normal. Because of this, I had three things that made a huge difference in my life.

Firstly, I could fail and fail and fail and fail, and it would be okay. Secondly, I learned that If I did wrong or crossed a boundary, there would be repercussions. Life has laws and rules. Sometimes we need to redefine the rules and test them but never in a way that hurts others. And lastly, which was most important, we learned to forgive ourselves for our shortcomings very quickly. My parents never held a grudge or punished us for something more than once. We got the punishment and the lesson, and they left it there, until the next time we did wrong. What a difference it made.

Our relationship with our self is the most important relationship we will have in life. Having that self-love will give us the strength and kindness needed to weather life's storms. A lot of our self-love and self-worth was fostered when we were young. We then went through life sculpting that self-love in our interactions with others and with ourselves — sometimes in good ways and sometimes in destructive ways. It's never too late to learn the self-love that you seek. Practice being kinder to yourself. You are worthy and deserving of love.

Not everyone was born with the kind of parents I have, nor should it matter. So long as you are able to break down the messaging you received as a child to make sense of it right or wrong you can grow. Some of you were born to a single mother or father, or to parents that punished you for everything you did. Some of you had parents who neglected you or taught you in a way that they were taught from their parents, right or wrong.

All of this was out of your control, yet it can still play a huge role in your life. I've seen successful people who were beaten into submission, either by their parents or by life circumstances, but who carry bitterness with their success. Many of you may still deal with the trauma of something that happened to you as a child. It's time to heal that trauma and learn to forgive yourself. Our upbringing was not of our choosing, we have to do the best we can with the hands that we were dealt. Living a motivated and happy life is about freeing ourselves of trauma and pain.

Many of us, throughout our childhoods, were scolded each time we fell short. Rather than being taught how to do better, we had parents who would use negative reinforcement to scare us into doing better. In all my years as a youth worker, I have found that positive reinforcement works much better at getting results than using fear. Positive reinforcement is finding the positives in a situation as opposed to focusing on the negatives. Telling a young child that you are extremely disappointed in their grades at school will most probably build sadness and destroy self-esteem.

A child wants nothing more than to receive their parents' love and acceptance. The grade at school is nowhere near as important in the long-term success of a child as their self-esteem. Now, this isn't about sugar coating everything, but it is about being very mindful of the messaging that we give children. It is also about understanding the messages that we were given when we were young.

Were there times in your life that you distinctly remember something a parent or teacher said that stuck with you? It could have been a single message said whilst that parent was having a bad day that affected you for many years. Are you aware, or have you articulated, what those specific messages were? Chances are, if not exposed, they can still have a subconscious effect on your self-esteem or sense of self.

The most motivated people of all time have quite literally failed their way to success. It is safe to say that failing is really a step on the path to succeeding. This is from Hollywood stars to political influencers and sporting greats. When we look at their lives what we first see are their accomplishments and accolades. When we dig deeper, we find years of struggle and failure. You could do research into many of your personal heroes just to prove this fact. Because their reasons for success (why statement) were so strong, they decided to get up every single time they failed and try again. They acknowledged their failures, learned from their mistakes, and then forgave themselves quickly.

Humans are very good at staying in a place of self-loathing and blame. We think about the same problem or mistakes often weeks, months, or years after we made them. We look at our mistakes from every angle possible, and we do it over and over. We assume that going over the same thing a thousand times will bring some new answer or new clarity to our issues. Do you have situations in your life that you waste vital energy running through your mind constantly? Circumstantial things which are mainly out of your control? It's time to let them go.

Essential to finding and maintaining motivation is being able to forgive ourselves for mistakes and failures. Why? Because staying in a negative mindset over things that lived in the past can only negatively influence our future. The guilt that you hold or the pain that you caused needs to be released. You've punished yourself long enough for your mistakes.

If we can accept the fact that any decision we made at a time was with the best of our knowledge, then we can come to peace with decisions that led to negative outcomes. Learning from them and deciding not to repeat them has great power in life. And if for lapse of judgement we make the same mistake, then once again, we should forgive ourselves quickly and try again.

The process of forgiveness starts internally, and then it will manifest in an abundance of positive outcomes and motivation. We will no longer be focused in on what we did wrong, but on what we can now do right.

The way to look at failure is how we would look at a summit attempt on Mt Everest — the world's tallest mountain. The air at the top of Everest is so thin that even with oxygen canisters, climbers need to acclimatize in stages. A climber does not just get to base camp and then walk up the mountain. They move from base camp one to two. They then acclimatize and move to three, etc. A lot of the time, they may even go backwards from camp three back to camp two as part of this process. And if for whatever reason they can't make a final and safe summit attempt, they return the next season. And thus is the process of failing our way to being successful and motivated. Sometimes we must take that step backward in order to move forward.

Motivation needs a clean mental space. Our motivation cat doesn't return if the room is full of angry dogs. And so our failures and mistakes need to be learned from and removed quickly to allow motivating thoughts back into our head.

Forgive others but also forgive yourself. When you zoom right out and look on your life from the grander picture, your mistakes and failures become minuscule. Love yourself, be kind to yourself even when you don't believe you deserve that kindness. The truth is that we all deserve compassion, kindness, love, and forgiveness. We are all here doing our best with what we have.

Pita Taufatofua

Always Finish — Always Finish Strong

*"The end of a race is where our future is forged.
Always finish, always finish strong."*

It's a strange feeling I have writing this last chapter for you. On one hand, I am sad that our shared motivation journey is coming to an end and on the other, I am excited for you and the life that you are about to embark on. I never thought I would get emotional writing a book. It has been one of my life passions to share the knowledge of what I have learned, and I hope that you can take something from this that will benefit the rest of your life.

I'm sure that when you opened the first pages of this book, you were seeking tips on how to get motivated and I hope that what you found instead was a better understanding of self. Maybe you thought that motivation was about learning new things but found that it was also about unlearning old things. I wish I could tell you that change will always be easy, but it won't be. Anything of value in life will require you to put in a large amount of work. That is the price you have to pay to reach the next level. But don't let that deter you. You are capable and deserving of that next level.

I have two more stories which I would like to finish our little journey with. One is about finishing strong, and one is about the Olympic spirit.

My hardest race before qualifying for the Winter Olympics took place in Poland. The track was steep and narrow with hills that felt like they never ended. We arrived the day before the race, and I felt something wasn't quite right. My friend Yona along with many excellent skiers were falling on the very narrow and fast bends. I was given the number 13 skier's bib and started the race. I got to the top of the first big hill after a tough climb, my legs were already shaking. On the way down the hill, I got caught in a sharp, packed-snow turn, and my ski binding broke, sending my ski all the way down the hill I had just climbed and into the forest. I took off my remaining ski and ran after it. I eventually found it and returned up the hill.

I had already lost fifteen minutes of precious time needed to keep pace with the winning skiers and was still on my first lap of a six-lap race. I have a saying that you should always turn up, and you should always finish what you start and finish strong. There was no way I was going to get the qualifying time I needed to make the Olympics in that race. But I had to finish. I used a shoelace and tied my ski to the binding and around my boot to hold it on. I continued the race and fell over fifteen times on the hard track. Each time I would fall, my face would scrape along the ice as my skis went in different directions. I would have to stand back up, compose myself and continue on. I rarely ever fell in a race.

By the time I reached my last lap, I was forty-five minutes behind the winner, and everyone had left except the last officials; they were packing up the stadium. Waiting at the finish line were Yona and Madrazo, my friends from Chile and Mexico. With my last push of energy, I finished the race, with a sprint against no one but myself, and collapsed. I knew that I had to finish, and I had to finish strong. If I didn't, then I would take that into other areas of my life.

Pita Taufatofua

Whatever adventures you embark on, always finish, and always finish strong. Never underestimate yourself and your potential to do great things. I can't stress how important finishing is for your mind and for your future.

The irony was that the race In Iceland, where I eventually qualified for the Olympics, also had given me the number 13 skier's bib to wear. My worst race and my best race had that same number. I knew that the number meant nothing and all that mattered was that I had self-belief. Your motivated and happy life isn't about the external factors but about you nurturing and feeding the self-belief you need to always finish and to always finish strong.

I have tears coming down my face as I write this. At the age of twenty-one, I wasn't sure about my life purpose. I knew I wanted to become an Olympian, but it wasn't working out, and I was struggling in all areas of life. I walked into the university library one afternoon and found a VHS tape on the Olympic dream. I played that tape in a quiet corner of the library.

In it, I saw Olympians defy the most difficult odds to be able to compete and call themselves an Olympian. There were athletes whose legs were trembling under the race conditions of a marathon yet continued forward. Some, tired with fatigue would crawl to the finish line. Other competitors were competing despite broken bones. I sat there in that quiet corner with tears running down my face. I felt the strength of those Olympians and the human spirit's power to overcome adversity.

I knew then that my purpose was to find a way despite the odds to become an Olympian and to teach people how they too could become Olympians in their field of life. That they too had the courage and heart to overcome their challenges and their fears. You may have reached this point and still not know your life purpose or the meaning for your life. That is okay.

Keep moving forward and keep your heart open to learning and you will find that meaning when the time is right. Use the steps you have learned to help you create good habits. Motivation and a happy life are about returning back to your center, to your foundation. Trust that you can achieve any dream that you set your heart and mind to.

I always thought that life was about achieving goals. The truth I found is that your greatest and most valued rewards will rarely be the goals that you seek. Your true happiness will come from the people that you meet, the love that you share and the experiences you have on your quest to achieve your dreams. Your Olympic Gold will be the new person that you become — a person full of self-love, strength, and limitless potential.

With much love and positivity, I wish you the best on your motivation and life journey.

"Ofa lahi atu,"

Pita Taufatofua

"The Motivation Station"

Pita Taufatofua

Gratitude

Very little in my life would have ever been accomplished without the love and support of key people over many years. I hope one day to pay back, or forward, the kindness you have shown me. I am eternally grateful to you all.

To God - Thank you for showing me that all things are possible. For loving me despite my shortcomings and for being my foundation in troubled times.

My Parents - My greatest gift was being born to you and nurtured by you. Thank you for the lessons you have given me. There is a large part of you in the words of this book.

To my older brother Chris - You were always there when I needed you. I'm glad you were born before me. I couldn't do half the job you have done in taking care of us.

To my older sister Langi - You show me every day the patience and kindness needed to be an amazing Parent and Sister as you raise your beautiful kids. I am in awe of you.

To my older sister Wendy - I wish I had got to spend more time with you. You are still here in our hearts and always will be.

To my younger brother Nik - Seeing how happy you were when you married the love of your life will always be one of my most treasured moments. Thank you for leading the way.

To my younger sister Luisa - You truly are the Sunshine in the hearts of everyone you meet. Being around you inspires me to life a happy life and to share that joy with others.

To my youngest brother JT - Watching you grow into the amazingly smart, strong, articulate, and generous man you are has been something that inspires me every day.

To my coaches Master Paul and Thomas Jacob - Thank you for never giving up on my dream to become a dual Olympian, for believing when others doubted. The best is yet to come.

To my friends and family - Thank you for all your patience, understanding, and guidance in helping shape who I am today. There is a little bit of all of you in this book in one form or another. I value each and every one of you in a unique and special way.

To my past love - Thank you for the memories and all the great times. Without you, I could never have seen the areas I needed to improve and grow. My heart has nothing but love and gratitude for your place in my life.

To my support team who helped make this book possible:

To Ty -Your friendship, support, patience and strength through adversity inspires all you meet. Your gift needs to be shared with the world. You will always have family with the Taufatofuas'.

To my readers - Alex, German, April, Cate, Gail, and Pila- Your input has been priceless and helped me go deep into my understanding of all things I thought I knew.

To my final editor Victoria Mace - It takes a special and patient person to show me the difference between then and than, or effect and affect. And an even more special person to have the patience to spend a month debating the use of an Oxford comma with me. I am excited to see all the good things that are coming your way.

To the International Olympic Committee - Thank you for showing the world the power of the Olympic spirit in bringing people from all walks of life together. I am honored to be called an Olympian, and I will continue to share that spirit with the world.

To my Tongan and Polynesian Ohana - Thank you for showing me how to be happy with nothing but the people around you. Thank you for your humility and your ongoing support.

And finally,

To all the young people in the homeless shelters I worked with - I wish I could have given back as much knowledge and patience as you gave me. Thank you for teaching me the power of the human spirit to overcome adversity. I will continue to honor you all by sharing that message with the world.

I value your messages of support. Should you wish to stay connected with me, or to assist the Pita Foundation in providing opportunities to young people of the Pacific, while bringing awareness to the health of our oceans and planet, then head to:

www.TeamPita.com

About the Author

Pita Taufatofua is an expert at achieving the Impossible.

An Olympian of the highest caliber, he has competed in both the Summer and Winter Olympic Games despite the odds. He is the first UNICEF Goodwill Ambassador to the Pacific, where, using his notoriety for good, he helps address children's access to health and education services, while advocating for their rights worldwide. His work in homeless shelters for over fifteen years has a proven track record for assisting young people to succeed where they had lost hope. He has spoken on motivation at the U.N. at the request of Mr. Miroslav Lajčák of Slovakia, former President of the General Assembly, and alongside Canadian Prime Minister, Justin Trudeau, for Solve at MIT, the annual summit addressing solutions for global challenges. He's broken the internet twice as the Tongan Flag Bearer and plans to be a superhero for the people and our planet. He's done it all, intends to do more, and continues to inspire millions.

Made in the USA
Middletown, DE
04 March 2020